Life Writing Series / 6

Life Writing Series

In the **Life Writing Series,** Wilfrid Laurier University Press publishes life writing and new life-writing criticism in order to promote autobiographical accounts, diaries, letters and testimonials written and/or told by women and men whose political, literary or philosophical purposes are central to their lives. **Life Writing** features the accounts of ordinary people, written in English, or translated into English from French or the languages of the First Nations or from any of the languages of immigration to Canada. **Life Writing** will also publish original theoretical investigations about life writing, as long as they are not limited to one author or text.

Priority is given to manuscripts that provide access to those voices that have not traditionally had access to the publication process.

Manuscripts of social, cultural and historical interest that are considered for the series, but are not published, are maintained in the **Life Writing Archive** of Wilfrid Laurier University Library.

Series Editor
Marlene Kadar
Humanities Division, York University

Memoirs from Away: A New Found Land Girlhood

Helen M. Buss / Margaret Clarke

Wilfrid Laurier University Press

[WLU]

We acknowledge the support of the Canada Council for the Arts for our publishing program. We acknowledge the financial support of the Government of Canada through the Book Publishing Industry Development Program for our publishing activities.

Canada

Canadian Cataloguing in Publication Data

Buss, Helen M. (Helen Margaret)
  Memoirs from away : a new found land girlhood

(Life writing ; v. 6)
ISBN 0-88920-350-4

1. Buss, Helen M. (Helen Margaret). 2. Newfoundland – Social conditions – 20th century.* 3. Women authors, Canadian (English) – 20th century – Biography.* I. Title. II. Series.

PS8025.B87A3 1999   C818′.5409   C98-9324541-6
PR9183.B87A3 1999

Front cover concept and photograph by Sandra Woolfrey. Cover watercolour illustration by Mathias Guenther. Cover design by Leslie Macredie.

∞

Printed in Canada

for
Kathleen and Harold Clarke
who made me
and Richard Buss
who lets me be

Contents

Foreword

Shortly after the last of my babies was born in 1973, I began to write. And as I wrote and wrote and wrote I formed in my mind the conviction that if I ever published anything I would use my middle and maiden names, Margaret Clarke, as my writing name. It wasn't that I didn't like my first and married names—Helen Buss—it was just that the writing felt like it was reaching for some other identity, one lost or not yet found. This feeling about naming was so intense that I started to practice the name Margaret Clarke on all sorts of private scraps of paper, inside the covers of three ring binders left over from night classes and on spare name tags from past teaching workshops, the kind that have typed at the top, "Hello, my name is. . . ." I would fill in the words "Margaret Clarke." When I discovered that Margaret meant "pearl" in Greek, I developed elaborate fantasies about going to a Greek island and finding my true identity, my lost pearl of a self. But since Helen Buss had children to raise, a career to make and a husband to live with, the idea of an island paradise receded. Instead of escaping to an island I wrote. Early in the 1980s I completed a novel, *The Cutting Season*, which won a writing prize in Manitoba.

At the same time I had also embarked on a career as an academic writer, having begun a graduate degree in English at the University of Manitoba. One of my teachers was the distinguished writer and scholar Robert Kroetsch, who incidentally was on the jury that had awarded the prize to my novel. He told me he almost fell off his chair when he was told that the author they had selected, Margaret Clarke, was in real life his student, Helen Buss. "I just could not imagine you were the person who wrote that book," he told me. He suggested that since I was beginning to publish academic articles under the name Helen M. Buss, I had better think about the problem of my two names: "Having two names is going to be trouble," he warned. He was right. Not only right about the practical difficulties involved in writing under two names, but right in terms of his implication that Margaret Clarke and Helen Buss represented very different qualities.

I used to think that Helen Buss was the sensible, practical woman who held down a teaching job, studied for a Ph.D. and raised kids. I used to think Margaret Clarke was my inner child, the imaginative part of me that needed to be hidden, protected from a cruel world. I used to feel that when I collapsed in uncharacterisitc tears and anger, or when I was unduly wounded by criticism, it was little Margaret Clarke who wasn't as tough-skinned as Helen Buss. I used to think that Helen was the academic writer and Margaret the imaginative writer. Nowadays, I do not believe that the two parts of me are as far apart as I used to think. Nor are the two kinds of writing. What has convinced me is the realization that I could not have dared any of the imaginative steps I needed to take in my academic work without the Margaret side of me, nor could I have made my stories without the Helen part of me that has studied the literary tradition inside which I work.

Today, as I write, I think that these two identities were merely the way I have named the process that all of us go through in growing up. We learn to suppress the parts of ourselves that are not acceptable to the ideologies inside of which each of us lives. These hidden and under-developed parts of ourselves will make themselves felt nevertheless, and sometimes very negatively. They may be suppressed, repressed, even oppressed, folded away in crannies of the brain we hardly ever visit, but they are still present somewhere on the spiraling of human identity that is each of us. As this spiral of the self is tossed through and around time and experience, those hidden qualities push toward con-sciousness, unfolding strangely and when we least expect or want them. They plague us with eccentricity, dysfunction, even illness, pleading for a place in the world. I believe that the existence of a forbidden self has to do with a multiple of variables, such as our family, our class, our race, our country, factors that affect each of us differently depending on our talents, our predispositions and the events of our lives. I don't think it is possible for anyone to grow up, in any culture, without denying some self-potential in order to fit in. For me, gendering has played a large part in allowing many abilities to remain neglected.

It just goes to show that Adam's God was right when he told his number one man to name things. Naming does give you power over creation. The minute I named Margaret Clarke as a working part of me, writing became possible. However, the more I write under the two names, the more I feel the need to bring together the so-called fictional and non-fictional worlds they represent. This has been happening for some time now. Although my two novels have fictional plots, my short stories have had unacknowledged factual locations in my own life. One of my favourite creations, my play *Gertrude and Ophelia*, could not have been written by Margaret Clarke if Helen Buss had not been studying for her Ph.D. and needed to rebel a little under the weight of all those male writers on her university-approved reading lists. As my years in the academy go by, I find that the more I develop my skills as an academic writer the more I need the imaginative reworking of material from my own life to facilitate my critical essays and books. This desire to admit that my whole self is involved in all my writing and the desire to witness to all I have learned as a female person have led to my decision to write memoirs rather than a novel or a scholarly text. This desire for the self that is joined to all the others and the otherness that makes me who I am, leads me to sign myself:

Traverse Bay   Helen Buss / Margaret Clarke
Summer 1997

Acknowledgments

A memoir is a long time growing. As it grows it borrows from the lives of many people and many people nurture it, some of them without knowing that they do so. For example, in 1981 when I published my very first story, "The Education of Child," in *Manitoba Stories*, the writer Sandra Birdsell was generous in her comments on my work and told me that the main character "Child" was worth writing a longer book about, maybe even a novel. I've found that my childhood self could not become a novel, but instead she became part of these memoirs. So in a sense this book has been growing for all these years and learning from many lives.

I would like to especially acknowledge the help of the following people:

I thank my birth family, both immediate and extended, for being the articulate Newfoundlanders that they are and for letting me share in their lives through their lively conversations, their jokes and their stories. I thank my children for making themselves at home in various locations in Canada and showing me, once again, that the Canada I imagined as a child, may indeed be possible.

I am especially grateful to my cousin Robin Peet and his wife Trudy Peet for their hospitality on more than one occasion and for helping us see the Avalon. I am grateful for the fish dinner and the reminiscences that followed at the home of my cousin Jean Power and her husband Len Power.

I am appreciative of the efforts of the staff of the Curriculum Materials Centre, Faculty of Education, Memorial University for the time they took to help me with my research.

I am indebted to Elizabeth Peters and Ross Peters for showing me a part of Newfoundland I did not know and for Elizabeth's letters that keep me connected to Newfoundland even though I am from away.

I would like to thank Dr. Neil Mowchun for the very professional manner in which he helped me to do the difficult work of discovering my forbidden self.

In the writing of this book I have received invaluable suggestions and guidance from Sandra Woolfrey, Director of Wilfrid Laurier University Press, and the readers for the Press, as well as from Marlene Kadar, the editor of the Life Writing series.

I am grateful to the Department of English, University of Calgary, where I work in an academic environment that provides me with many enrichments for both my scholarly and creative endeavours. During part of the time I was writing these memoirs my scholarly research on the memoir form was funded by the Social Sciences and Humanities Research Council of Canada. The articles and papers that I continue to write based on that research have contributed to this writing also, so that the scholarly and the creative truly have come together for me.

Finally, I would like to thank Richard Buss, my fellow traveller, for his close reading.

Introduction

I have come to Victoria, British Columbia, as I do for a week each February, to read the memoirs and personal papers of pioneer women whose manuscripts are kept here in the public archives. But from the moment I arrive my first thought is not about my research, but about writing an introduction to the memoir stories that have cropped up like wild flowers among my other writing. I wrote the first drafts of these memoirs in Florida, that paradise of remembrance where everyone comes from somewhere else, where Canadians can feel really Canadian because they miss listening to the CBC. I visit Florida often because my parents have an apartment by the sea and some time ago, when I had a year of study leave, they lent it to me for several months so I would have a quiet place to work away from the Canadian winter.

Spending an extended time in Florida, I found myself writing about the Canadian identity that I adopted, or that adopted me, as a seven-year-old Newfoundlander; the American difference reminded me constantly of what it was to be Canadian. Being Canadian is real in Florida, because you know you are not American, whereas here in Victoria, in my own country so to speak, I often find myself uncomfortable, as if I were a Newfoundlander from the old-time outports in a merchant's town parlour.

The invention of my Canadian identity began when I was a very little girl, the day after the referendum votes of adult Newfoundlanders were finally all counted and we became part of the Canadian nation. My father and the history books tell me that our coming to Canada was a much more complex process than I remember, with run-off elections and weeks of getting in the outport vote that finally tipped the scales

1

toward a decision that most of the city folk of St. John's did not want. The tentative announcements gradually became real only over days, weeks. But I remember it differently.

In my remembering it all happens one late night, in our living room at our home on Craigmillar Avenue, with my father's friends smoking cigars around my mother's folding card-table, its surface strewn with maps and statistics. My father made predictions, while others denied their validity; it was an intense male world which my mother stayed well away from, and which I watched through the glass-panelled doors that looked into that room full of men. These are the kind of moments memory's imagination shapes for its myth of the self; all time delays, all non-essentials of character and plot fall away and only the archetypal necessities of identity remain: the mother in the kitchen, the father's world behind the little squares of glass, and later, my territory, the garden under the maple trees.

The maples had been planted by my father many years before, when he could not have known of their aptness for my secret Confederation ritual. That morning, after his night of cigar smoke and statistics, he told me I was now indeed a Canadian. Or perhaps it was later, after the negotiations that he had shared in, helping to get the best deal possible for the future of communications in Newfoundland. Anyway, it was some morning after, whenever it was, that I stood under the maples and turned around and around, facing each of the four corners of my world, saying aloud, "I am a Canadian; I am a Canadian; I am a Canadian; I am a Canadian." I greeted each point of the compass, there in the dizzy pleasure of my turning, not knowing what travail I was taking on.

Some days now I feel like the only Canadian. Some days I feel like the last Canadian. Some days I feel that being a Canadian is impossible. I like to think that all of these feelings are essential to being a Canadian. Every Canadian must feel this alone. All Canadians must feel that their own personal history is the one that makes them Canadian and since no one else has had quite the same history, they live alone in their Canadian identity. When we talk of being Canadian we speak not of national myths, but of our own lives. To be a Canadian is to be an autobiographer.

Now, a lifetime later, I am here on the island at the other end of Canada looking at apartment condominiums, playing with the prairie dweller's dream of retiring "to the coast." My bread and butter is back in Calgary, where the messages pile up in my mailbox and on my e-mail at the university, and my job awaits, as secure as anything academic can be in the Province of Alberta. Alberta feeds me well, but does not make me feel at home; something about its efficiency, its wealth, the smoothness of a politics that aims always at an unproblematic optimism, makes me feel unreal. Each summer I pack my research notes, full of the anonymous stories of women gathered in Canadian archives from Victoria to Ottawa, and travel back to Manitoba, the place where I made my marriage, raised my children, became that thing we call, in an ancient and strange phrase, a doctor of philosophy. Better to call me a doctor of memoirs, a job description you won't find a lot of call for in the classifieds. At any rate, the province I have spent most of my adult life in, Manitoba—decades after coming there because of my father's job prospects—had no job for the "doctor" I had become. And so I went away again. Once more westward.

But the Manitoba that will not hold me still holds a small piece of real Canadian territory dear to me, the always-unfinished cottage on the shore of Lake Winnipeg, the place that has been ours for the last quarter century. In these times, that is a long time. The pine walls of its interior, shaped by my husband Richard, are full of my changes. Each summer, as I work my research inside them, they declare my history and its lessons: "don't you get too high-falootin' girl, with your doctorate and your professorship; remember the woman's life that feeds it. Remember all the diapers and dishes and Tuesday-evening suppers prepared on the run before night classes in Middle English, all the bittersweet poems of wifehood and the comfort stories for children alarmed in the night, remember all the lies and truths you had to tell yourself and others in order to learn about language in this place." Each summer Manitoba grounds me, centres me, makes me feel real for awhile.

When I began my study leave, I came to Manitoba for the summer to write and read, before heading for Florida in the late fall. I began to conceive of a trip to Newfoundland at the end of the year, a kind of reward for working hard. Maybe that's what caused the memoir stories to begin. I had been back to my birthplace only twice since I left in 1955. The first time, in 1969, I went with Richard, two kiddies and a truck and camper. We touristed through Prince Edward Island, along the Cabot Trail and spent five days in Newfoundland. My mother's sister, Aunt Helen, whom I am named after, was alive then and was good to me as she had always been. My father's brother, Uncle Leonard, had become the owner of my childhood home and he invited us to the best dinner of fresh salmon I have ever eaten. I went alone to walk through the neighbourhood. Standing by the familiar graveyard just south of our home, for the first time in my life of busy wifing, mothering, teaching—a life in which I felt all too real—I felt like a ghost haunting a former life. I remember not liking that feeling. It was the beginning, I think, of being overly conscious of my disconnectedness from my own lived life, the uneasy way you have to feel in order to be driven to words, driven by desire for those small moments when, writing, you live inside your own experience, your own body.

I avoided Newfoundland for over two decades after that time, finally going in the early nineties in the guise of researcher—a comfortable otherness—in search of women's stories. Every place I looked, I found the stories belonged to someone else; they were not mine. Cousins were kind, hospitable, but I did not feel at home. They had lives in this place; I did not. Generous with memory and talk, in the way Newfoundlanders are, my Aunt Jean took time out from dying of cancer to remember my childhood. We spent an hour together and when we said goodbye, I knew I would not see her again. She would be a memory, like my Aunt Helen and Aunt Thelma, the women whose stories had enlivened my childhood years.

Discouraged by not finding a suitable topic for research, depressed by the passing of so many in my parents' generation, whose lives had been Newfoundland for me, I opted for being a tourist, searching each day a different arm of the Avalon Peninsula, as if I were a lady from Manitoba, here to take slides to show my kids during the long prairie winter. For a few days I imagined that I was the mother of such a tightly knit prairie family, not the mom of grown children living thousands of kilometres from where home used to be. Several times we drove the circle of my childhood territory, the limits of my walking and bike-riding in old St. John's: west along Military Road where it becomes Harvey Road up by the Catholic Cathedral, past the place where I used to go to Holloway School, past where the street becomes LeMarchant Road, past the building which used to be Prince of Wales College, my school from grades six to nine, along to where LeMarchant becomes Cornwall Avenue and then down the hillside of Craigmillar Avenue, past my house to Topsail Road, down Water Street, along the harbour and up King's Bridge Road to our bed and breakfast near the new version of the Newfoundland Hotel. Each time we drove the circle I would remark on how the old St. John's seemed lost in the larger city built since my childhood. Each time I would marvel that the limits of my childhood took only twenty minutes to circle in our car. Each time Richard would slow down near my house on Craigmillar (now not owned by our family) and ask if I wanted a photograph, if I wanted to get out and walk around the neighbourhood. Each time I refused; it was too cold; it was too windy: it was ghosting time again. Months later, when I saw the photograph he took of me leaning against the *Peter Pan* statue in Bowring Park, I realized how hard it must have been to be with that woman in Newfoundland, her face full of her loss, her fear, her anger: a woman haunted by unmade stories. How could he have stood it?

This would be my third time back and I promised myself, as my study year continued and the stories started to happen, that this time would be different. One of the things that would make it different was the fact that my childhood friend Eleanor had re-entered my life. Ironically, in one of those fifteen minutes of fame that not very well-known writers get when someone decides they will make a convenient one-column feature in a national magazine, Eleanor had seen my picture and wrote asking if I could possibly be the Helen (Margaret) Clarke she grew up with. We exchanged histories, wrote letters over a year and finally arranged a reunion when both of us found ourselves in Europe at the same time. We met in Copenhagen and had such a good time that we agreed to meet again in Newfoundland. So this time there would be Eleanor to make me feel less unreal in Newfoundland. This time there would be a present moment in Newfoundland, especially since, as my plans grew, my parents decided to join us; I would be taking my mom and dad, Kathleen and Harold, home with me.

Harold and Kathleen have been home dozens of times since they left with their five children in tow to move to the Prairies in 1955; they have seen the changes in their home place, watched the growth of highways and suburbs and shopping centres, seen their Newfoundland and their generation gradually disappear. They admire the progress, mourn the deaths. Now they are getting a little too fragile to go on their own, so they will fly to St. John's where Richard and I will meet them. Their plans are simple, a week at their favourite bed and breakfast with their son-in-law and daughter to take them to all the old places that are part of them, and the few living folk they love, then off to Nova Scotia, where there is a sister, a son and daughter-in-law, and a granddaughter to visit. My own plans are more complex. Since these memoirs have begun to grow, I have become ambitious for material. I plan with a singleness of focus that only a writer bent on inspiration can.

My plans quickly become massive enough for a Russian novel. I will travel back over the territory of my life, all my Canadas, from my research into the past in Victoria, through the Calgarian present, to a month of reflection and preparation at the Manitoba cottage. Heading eastward we will stop first at the mill town in Northern Ontario where I began my teaching career, then take the Great Lakes route to Toronto to see my daughter and join the family, now mostly settled in southern Ontario, for my mother's eightieth birthday. After swallowing half a continent, we will visit my brother Hal and his family in Cleveland and absorb a chunk of America on the way to the Maritimes. My appetite for Canada regrets that we cannot taste Montreal and our French connection, my Aunt Denise, who graciously married my Uncle Jack a few decades back so that we could have Québécois cousins, but we are taking the American route to the Maritimes where our eldest son has settled, and to Halifax where my youngest brother will take us to Peggy's Cove and we will deep-breath some sea air, readying our palates for our Newfoundland destination. Yes, I was ambitious for this writing.

But ambition makes fools of writers. A couple of weeks before our departure I am explaining our itinerary to Richard—it seems I have not let him in on all the details of the Russian novel—when he suggests that we go by airplane instead of attempting such a long drive. I brush aside his concerns with distance; this is a symbolic journey, not to be contaminated with thoughts of the actual size of the continent. And haven't we already savoured half of America and Canada in our year of study and travel? Didn't we successfully drive to Florida in the fall, and in spring cross the south and west of the whole of the United States of America? Hadn't we picnicked by the Rio Grande, tasted the wine valleys in California, supped a full month on the archives in Victoria? Weren't we the intrepid pair who had gloriously flown to France for academic papers and more wine valleys? Weren't we the stubborn Canadians who single-handedly mastered the Paris subway system to return again and again to the Spanish embassy to win visas, despite turbot wars and bureaucracy, in order to get lost in the slums of Barcelona on our way to drink deeply of Gaudi and Miró? Hadn't we gorged on auto-routes at 140 clicks per hour, and bitten off forbidden pictures of the Mona Lisa? Hadn't we gobbled up two continents already this year? What was another 10,000 kilometres? Besides, driving to Newfoundland would be fun. What I wanted to tell Richard was that it would be part of my research and therefore sacred, but I knew by the doubt in his eye that such an argument was out.

So I bargained instead. I said I would do all the driving (a promise I had no intention of keeping), if he would have cruise control installed in the car. While I flew to Quebec City to give yet another paper our car was cruise-controlled. Days later, when my plane brought me back into the bright Winnipeg summer, I was still in a complete state of denial about the difficulty of travelling so far, after a year of trips. I had become addicted to motion. As I checked out the cruise control and arranged for final engine servicing, as I packed for whatever the next five weeks of journeying might bring, I kept telling myself that this was a culmination of the memoir writing, this was the trip into the past that would make all the writing real.

One hundred kilometres east of Winnipeg we quarrelled and Richard stopped speaking to me. A silence reigned which would rhythm our lives, with a few magical breaks, for the next eight months. The Russian novel now had both its war and its peace, for the silence had two opposite effects. On one hand, I could write no words. All my plans for diaries of documentation, of recording every precious feeling in every nook and cranny of the home place, of journalizing every meeting, be it with a person or a rock, failed me. Instead, it took great concentration to formulate a public face each day, to let no part of the silence lap over into the planned itinerary, to behave decently with family and friends. The few intense moments of angry lashing at the silence—an hour of frenzy and cruel words on the Pennsylvanian Turnpike, a night of tears in a New Brunswick motel room—took enormous energy. And they hurt. They hurt him and they hurt me. War between partners is hell. On the other hand, when it takes the form of silence, it also has an ironic peace, the peace of an intense aloneness.

I have just read these last paragraphs aloud to my husband. I have given him fair warning of this portrayal, this betrayal. All these memoir stories of mine are betrayals of the first rule of family life as we have shaped it in the last five hundred years. They are a betrayal of privacy. For better or for worse we have made a separate world of the family, pretending its commerce has no place in the exchanges of power and person that we call the public world. These memoirs, many women's memoirs, subvert this division. I know this. It is my business to know this. I cannot pretend I did not know I was betraying them all, all my family. I have tried to keep it as clean a betrayal as possible, tried to acknowledge that these are my own constructions, not their lives, tried to keep my own foolishness to the foreground. But as my older brother once told me, it's not very flattering to become a minor character in someone else's story. For everybody's sake, why don't I just call this a fiction and get on with it?

That last question was enough to keep me away from my word processing for a while. Here at the far western edge of Canada we go about, like a typical prairie couple, amazed once more at the Victoria trees blossoming in February and the blossoming prices of condominiums. The silence that came on the way to Newfoundland has just begun to fade away. Almost a year and we have decided to work at whatever our relationship is to be on the other side of this silence.

I am avoiding the question. Why insist on this referentiality to my own life? After all, as my academic colleagues would tell me, all writing is construction, all construction is some form of fiction. And I know what can happen when as an academic I construct even the conditional truths of literary theory. Like a lawyer, I tend to try to write a language so precise it becomes a secret code between initiates. And this desire to name genre, this effete play with the ancient word memoirs, my colleagues would rightly tell me, is prescriptive, a desire to impose, to fix, to dictate an order that writing continually seeks to overthrow. If I were a smarter academic I should have moved well beyond genre by now.

Across the road from my Victoria hotel window—at this very moment—the orderliness of stone arches, crowned cupolas and florid statuary, filtered by the sculpture of well-tended, well-placed fir and oak trees and the finishing detail of the Canadian flag, makes real the legislature of British Columbia. It is as constructed as this memoir. It is as fictional as this memoir. But every day millions of people expect that its order will make manifest their power as a people and make their lives more possible. Now that's the kind of genre I would like to get my hands on. That's the kind of memoir I had in my head before I began to write. And all I have achieved so far is this puzzlement about writing, this guilt about representing other peoples lives. Do the politicians across the road feel like this?

And I realize as I write that writing is always involved in stealing from other writers. It was Shelley, not me, who said that what he had written could never be a match to what he had conceived in his head. It was he who compared writers to legislators, saying writers were the true legislators of the world. Now, two hundred years later, I cannot write a word that I have not stolen from the fathers of literature, without a scene which I have not snatched from the lives of other people. Like the other Shelley, Mary, who knew all about the "fathers" of literature, I am afraid that all my art and science can never make more than a monster who cannot find a home, cannot find love.

Here I am, finally, letting my writing descend from apologia to apology before it has properly begun. And, yes, dear reader, I have to admit my apology is driven by my awareness of you. You know that feeling when you sense the possibility of an unfriendly judgment and you try to prevent it by apologizing first. I am very aware that you are reading this, perhaps more aware than I should be. I have to admit that ever since I began to write I have always imagined you and the more I write autobiographically the more I imagine you. This is not always considered a good thing for a writer. Some would say that a good writer writes for himself first, and then if there is an audience, well and good. But you are always on my mind, pumping my blood pressure up as I write, hurrying and slowing my fingers over the keys, and pressing me, sweating me, through the revisions. Perhaps this consciousness of you at the other end of this process comes from spending so many years being a mother and a teacher, knowing that words are acts which make and shape others. But you are not my child or my student. Perhaps I put you too much in the place of the parent. At any rate, from the first reader "feedback" I received early in my career as a writer, and on through my writing life, as the judgments of literary juries, critics, and readers came to me, I grew very aware of how powerful is the reader, how the reader makes my work into something else, into your own story. But in the long run I probably have my own desire to blame for my trepidation, because I want you to be so many readers. I want you to read with the total identification that I often find myself caught in as a reader. I want you to read with the distance of literary appreciation, alert for the subtle inside the simple. I want you to read as my mother, my sister, my friend. I want you to be every kind of reader, a multitude of readers; I am hungry for readers. I want you to admire me, I want you to love me, I want you to read me.

And all this is a bit of a stall, for if the truth, my truth, be known, I am realizing as I write that I cannot construct a return to my homeland in the satisfying way you and I might want it. It is not only because the experiences of that summer visit are too close in time, not yet possessed by some archaic place in my brain stem that is able to make a story of my past. It is also because I did not, and cannot return to my homeland. After four decades of living on the Prairies I am from "away" and therefore cannot come home. In Newfoundland "away" is the word they use to explain the crass, the ignorant or the merely mysterious acts inevitable to the condition of being foreign to a place: "Never mind the girl, she's from away," they would say with compassion. And I will always be from away. Even in that Manitoba cottage it is my husband's world that grounds me. The truth is, dear reader, that wherever I am I will always be from away. What happened to me in Newfoundland in that summer of returning was something between déjà vu and tourism, short moments of familiarity, small glimpses of people I might have been. These are all my writing is made of, that and a few lucky breaks and memory.

Speaking of lucky breaks, today I walked with my husband's brother by the narrows of Victoria's harbour, all the time wondering how I could write this introduction to my return to my birthplace. My companion exclaimed on the narrowness of the space, and the extremity of the turn the ships must make to come into Victoria's inner harbour. Being from the Prairies he likes a nice expanse of road, two wide ditches and a couple of fields to make a big turn.

"You should see the narrows of St. John's harbour," I tell him.

"Where?" says he.

"St. John's, Newfoundland."

"People live there?" He chuckles in the way of my husband's prairie family, as if humour were a slightly lascivious activity. I laugh with him, at his "Newfie" joke, for, without knowing it, he has given me my opening into my memoir stories, into my childhood, my girlhood on the Avalon Peninsula in Newfoundland.

People Live Here: Imagine That

Not my brother-in-law's words "people live *there*," but rather the phrase "people live here," kept crossing my mind on my return visit to my birthplace. Coming into Port aux Basques on a grey day deciding between rain and fog, we watched the long, low stretch of rock narrowing the barren grey of the sea between our ferry and landfall. Startled by the sudden appearance of dwellings rising unexpectedly in the momentary breaks of light, I am amazed that *people* live here! Yet there will be times on my visit when, as my mainland carefulness falls from my manner and my speech speeds to its childhood rate, and as other women with no reticence about expressing their opinions make me dare to be downright rude by prairie standards for middle-class females, that the phrase becomes joyous: "people *live* here." And in short seconds of forgetfulness I will almost feel at home; I come into possession of a keen desire to be one of the people who lives *here*.

The northern arm of Newfoundland points at an eastward angle northwards, and the road follows the shoreline so closely, the coastal land between the mountains to the east and the sea to the west rises so few feet above sea level, that you feel like you are floating in the water as you drive. The day we travelled north there was a sunny westerly wind and small whitecaps: glorious tourist weather. The small new-looking towns drifted by, reminding me that it was the twentieth century before Newfoundlanders finally really owned their west coast, formerly the "French" shore, reserved over centuries for the fishing of foreign nations. Up and down the coast there are remembrances of the civilizations that came, fought and left. At Port au Choix we scan the list of Amerindians and Inuits; at The Arches we imagine the canoes and

11

kayaks venturing across from the mainland; at L'Anse-au-Meadows we strain our eyes northward for the square of a Viking sail. It is pleasing to be a tourist and live in the stories of other people's history.

Newfoundlanders have a good thing going on the northern arm: from the quaintness of the Bonne Bay settlement, through the craggy ruggedness of Gros Morne park, to the serene clean landscape of grass and sea at L'Anse-au-Meadows, this is a tourist paradise. If they had Alberta's entrepreneurial savvy, they'd make the whole thing into a park, like the drive between Banff and Jasper, and maybe ship the people to some nice place like Corner Brook. But Newfoundlanders keep insisting on living here. They continue living in such places as Parson's Pond, Port Saunders and St. Anthony, where they have to keep reinventing their means of livelihood to have a reason to stay. Right now it would seem to be lobster and crab that keeps them.

But they are learning about the tourist trade too. My father had warned us that Newfoundlanders, outside the main centres, don't tend to go in for nice motels and pleasant restaurants. "They are not raised to be service sector people," he tells me. Then assertively he adds: "They do not like to serve." I see as we head north that this must be changing as new motels, brazen with vinyl siding and sea views, are cropping up in the villages. We are headed for the very northern tip of Newfoundland and to a hotel my dad has recommended. At the end of the highway we search all of St. Anthony for our hotel, missing the last hour the Grenfell Museum will be open that day, and still we cannot find our bed for the night. Finally we track it down twenty kilometres back the way we came. I have not stayed in such terrible accommodations since one night in Tucson, Arizona, when we suffered through a rattling air conditioner and eight lanes of highway right outside our window. Here it is beds that slope inward at the same angle as the Rocky Mountains and walls so thin that the neighbours' farts and burps are a cacophony magnified by the silence between Richard and I as we munch cheese and crackers for our dinner. We have ended up so far from town we can find no other food. The pure pleasure of the day's drive northward is lost in the stuffy heat of a room where the windows are sealed. Later, meeting my parents in St. John's, I described our experience to them and my father explained that we were in the wrong hotel, owing to our confusion of the word "Norse" with "Viking." When he discovered we had entirely missed seeing the museum dedicated to Dr. Grenfell's mission, he only shook his head like a Newfoundlander confronting someone from "away."

Much of my visit to Newfoundland was like that day in the north, moments of intense pleasure as the place and the people would make me forget I am a woman from away, followed by moments of loss, being lost, ending often in the terrible claustrophobia of waking late at night in some place that has no meaning for me. That is why, the next day, when my questions led our guide at L'Anse-au-Meadows away from the details of Norse settlement, and into the details of his own family's settlement, I urged his tangent on. With Richard and I both listening to him it was almost as if we were talking to each other. While we had lost the thread of our own plot, we could, for an hour, be held together by his story. Like most Newfoundlanders on the "French" shore, the family had only been there three generations. His children would be the fourth. His grandfather had come from the part of Newfoundland my own people were from, the Conception Bay area. He described the pioneer-like days of his own childhood, the activities of winter woodcutting and summer fishing that were his life. He mourned the coming of the highway, despite the fact that it brought the tourists that created his job, because it meant that the old community ties were weakened. He was an articulate, intelligent man and the first of my reminders of what I always tend to forget about Newfoundlanders: their exceptional ability to express what they think and feel.

It is not something I am used to anymore. In the daily places I live, people so often do not trust language to say what they mean, do not seem to know what they feel and refuse to speak what is on their minds. Conversation becomes a game in which we all try to mask ourselves from the other. Here, again and again, I meet people confident enough in the value of their own language-making, and in the listener's ability to hear them without perversion, that communication constantly startles me. Like some long lost endorphin circling a runner's brain, some substance would suddenly begin to zip through my chemistry and talk would begin to have meaning. These are moments when I forget I am from away and I almost feel I am from here.

Like the day we sailed to Julie's Cove with my old friend Eleanor and her husband Ron on their sailboat. Anchoring in the perfect circle of the cove, we go ashore and are guided through the undergrowth beyond the cove's beaches to find the now-deserted settlement which is marked only by a grassy bank where the houses would have been. Farther up the densely treed hill we read its story in the language of the graveyard's headstones. They tell us succinctly of brothers drowned, of wives dead in birthing and children taken by disease. No words are wasted. These bleached-white testaments tell the history of so much of Newfoundland, the brave, tenuous communities of interconnected families, the generations of lives spent in these small worlds of the coves, their ultimate diaspora. It would not be surprising if we were to meet someone from Sudbury or Seattle or Singapore climbing up through the underbrush to see her ancestors' graves. In the sunshine of the cove, as we watch the glitter of stones on the sea-floor below our boat, Eleanor makes a meal on a tiny stove in a galley that requires the ability to cook with only essential gestures, space being at a premium. She and Ron discuss the route home, how we might try a little sail despite the calm.

The next day, with better winds, we tack up and down the arm of ocean near their country home, and Eleanor lets Richard help her with the sails. Ron lets him hold the tiller. I am offered a chance, but refuse. Despite being born a Newfoundlander, this is my first experience of sailing. Each tack gets more ambitious in its reach, Ron helping Richard remember his sea cadet training, as we head closer and closer to shore on each turn. I am watchful of the precise and few words that construct the shared work of Ron as captain, Eleanor as crew, a world like the galley where only essential moves are permitted. At the end of one long tack, Eleanor, with a few words and a certain lift of the head and a look of coolness in the eyes that I seem to remember from decades ago, tells her husband to rein in his tacking, turn the boat farther from land. Later, safe at our moorage, as we gather our things to go ashore and our captain shows me how to secure the craft to the wharf, he explains their sailing partnership for the benefit of the feminist from away: "You see, Helen, while I am the captain, Eleanor is both crew and admiral."

Our burst of laughter at this moment becomes the theme of our visit, as people of the same age, although knowing nothing of each other for forty years or more, discover a generational economy, a similarity of taste in music and wine, in stories of child-rearing and hobbies, of words that have meaning for us because they are the words of people at our time of life, in our condition: us little ones born of the Depression and the War have made it to the end of the century, with our marriages intact (cross our fingers, knock on wood) with our children made into adults, and a decent portion of good health held onto in a country that still knows how to look after its elders (cross our fingers, knock on wood). We are lucky; we see that in each other and it makes us happy.

One evening after the sailing, after the wine and the dinner, the music and the talk, my husband smiles at me, the first sign that there may be a way through the silence that fell on the road to Newfoundland. It will be a long time before he smiles at me again, but I have had that smile, and I am willing to wait.

I begin to appreciate the privilege of my new silent marriage. I have returned to Newfoundland with a man who is a good driver, who will demand nothing of me and who will be, as always, a shield between me and the energy of my parents, leaving me free to discover the nature of "here" and "away."

The idea of walking in my old neighbourhood has, over the years, become mysteriously fearful. The memory of feeling like a ghost when I went there in my twenties, my refusal to set down my foot there when I had come a few years ago, had built a kind of anti-nostalgia in me: the dread that some carefully shaped identity would disintegrate by the very act of touching the ground. So this time I had deliberately booked us into rooms a few blocks distant from my home on Craigmillar Avenue to force myself to set foot in the neighbourhood. I wanted to face the ghosts, even if I was one of them. The first evening of our arrival in St. John's I went walking in the cemetery that had been both my childhood playground and my childhood terror. It is not well kept. I can remember when the caretaker who lived on the property had every path trimmed and all the fences in fine repair. Now his house is gone from its space on Topsail Road and the paths are unkempt and shabby. No kid would want to violate the rule of no bike-riding on these scruffy paths.

I walked all over the cemetery until it felt as ordinary to me as a backyard in need of a trim. I tramped down Topsail Road and up Craigmillar Avenue until every inch of my old grounds felt as unmagical as the streets of Calgary. One evening I walked past my house several times, surreptitiously glancing in the front windows as I did. Inside, people seemed to be having a dinner party. Talk and food and candlelight filled the dining room. How nice. How civilized. How good that the place is unhaunted by me, that life goes on in wonderful ordinariness without any notice of the middle-aged woman from the Prairies pausing on the street outside.

I confess that I turned toward my lodgings with a feeling of letdown that had not yet become relief. And then I saw the snails. Do you know that feeling when a memory long lost suddenly leaps full-blown in your head? It feels like a flower is blooming in your forehead, as in time lapse photography where the bud becomes a rose in a mere second of fecundity. The front of my head actually tingled as I bent down to examine the sidewalk in the late twilight. Yes, there they were, a dozen or so snails marching across the sidewalk, their delicate shellhouses, swirled brown and beige and white, carried delightfully on their backs as they went to and fro from whatever chore took them from the curb of the street to the cement and stone wall of the large garden of one of the more prosperous houses east of the cemetery.

When I was a child and became tired of all the playmates of my immediate neighbourhood, I would head east down Topsail Road towards the larger homes that marked a neighbourhood of slightly more prosperity, older trees, more established families. You might not notice the difference today, as these more spacious homes become old, their large gardens not kept to the old standards of my childhood. Along here, amongst the handful of "mansions," in a smaller, but still impressive home, lived a little girl whom I played with only rarely. I thought she was rich and so went to her house only when I was curious about the rich. This little girl (whose name escapes me) and I used to occasionally go and check on the snail settlement. There they would be, parading back and forth between street and garden wall. She and I would pick them up by their shells and carefully stroke their little tails, their creepy-crawly underbellies, and especially their little wiggling antennae. Oh, how that tickled our fancies, those soft, delicate wands, against our little girl fingers. Oh, how we shivered! Oh, how we laughed! We would play as gods with our little colony, lining them up one by one, or in ranks. We would turn them north when they wanted to go south, and south when they wanted north, and watch in amazement as they found their way back to whatever direction they intended before they were disturbed by the unseen fates, small girls bent on haunches, knees at our faces, intent on ordering the world of snails.

I remember one day the little girl told me that in France people ate snails. At first I was unbelieving, then, because she seemed so sure of her knowledge (she was, after all, rich), I was astounded, disgusted and worried in turn. "Would you eat snails?" I asked.

"Oh no," said she. "What would the garden do without them? They turn the soil you know." Sometimes, even if you are only six years old, you have enough sense to know when you are in the presence of poetry. And now the poetry of snails had survived the road changing from gravel to pavement, survived the pathway moving from foot-worn to concrete, and had gone on year after year in the same place for fifty years. They were here for me now, in the twilight, at the moment I had returned from away.

No longer comfortable on my haunches, I leaned against the garden wall and watched them for a while, feeling the flower of memory bloom in my head. I began to feel an amazing relief, then joy, that I had returned to such a scene of my childhood home. The snails have stayed with me, a scintillating visual image, from that moment to this, urging me on in these acts of memory.

Since the growing of images into similes and metaphors and the translation of them into symbols in my business, if this were a classroom instead of memoir I would probably ask my students to read the image of snails that carry their houses on their backs into a metaphor of the writer embodying language. Yet lately I find the working of language as symbol just a little embarrassing, the feeling I get when my students ask that inevitable question: "Did the writer really know that he was making all those different meanings? Did he really mean for us to see them?" More and more these days I want to stop my patient explanation about the complex relationship of writer, text and reader, stop my careful rhetoric of the importance of empowering ourselves to work with the complexity of language outside of authorial intention, and tell them that the use of metaphor and symbol is just a bad habit we have gotten into since we first came to believe that the word was somehow divine, that God was the word and the word was God. Symbolic language, I want to tell them, is all just the elaboration of an authoritarian belief system, outdated and oppressive. I do not tell them this because I know language has a tendency to become symbolic the moment we speak or write, like it or not, so we had better know how it keeps doing that, even when we are trying hard not to let it get away from us. I am trying hard right now.

But stumbling into the snail metaphor through this writing makes me realize once more the wavy line between memory and fact. Now that I reread what I have recounted to you as my memory of the snails and the little girl (whose name I still cannot remember), I realize much of it may be invented out of mere fragments of actuality. So, if you are one of the kids at the back of class who doubts the whole literary enterprise, here's my full confession. Yes, I can honestly testify that I used to play with snails at that spot on Topsail Road and I did know a little girl who—I suddenly remember at this moment of writing—came from a family who owned a jewellery store. I seem to remember her last name was Silver, but perhaps that would be too symbolically apt to be true. Whether or not I played in particular with her among the snails or with my brother or Eleanor or some unremembered child, or all of the above, is undecidable. I know someone told me about the French eating snails, and I think it happened while playing with the snails, and I do accurately remember (I think) being shocked. But you'll be relieved to know that my childhood was no more fanciful or poetic than any ordinary childhood and so the part about turning the soil and realizing poetry—well—that's just what decades of education in the literary tradition makes you do. Besides, isn't it worms that turn the soil? After an hour or so at my word processor, language just takes over, has its way with me. I'm sorry. I apologize.

One thing I can guarantee you: when I went to Newfoundland in the summer of 1995 and saw those snails on the sidewalk of Topsail Road just east of the cemetery I was one happy woman. It really did make me feel real in that place, driving out the fear of ghosts and old half-baked stirrings of who-knows-what traumas of childhood. Women writing today are encouraged to find dreadful things in their past. I was really happy to merely find the snails. My brow may not have quite tingled, but I slept well that night and seeing the snails made it easier to go about the Avalon Peninsula enjoying the old places, enjoying Harold and Kathleen's memories, without feeling I was a ghost with no solid flesh to hold my identity together. The snails "actualized" me as we would say today, and I am grateful for it. I hope nobody puts out slug poison in that garden and kills them before I get back to Newfoundland again. And I'm sorry I made up that eco-romantic line about turning the soil. So there you have it: confessions of a sometime fiction writer trying to walk the constantly moving line between what happened and what is made from what happened. Forgive me, for I was only trying to make things real. In compensation, let me tell you a story about my parents, one I will call "Harold and Kathleen in Newfoundland." My parents are so real, they're super-real.

The Newfoundland and Labrador tourist book has adopted for its motto the phrase that is a typical reaction of their citizens to any new fact, fancy or phenomenon: "Imagine that!" I can remember hearing the phrase constantly as a child. It seems to me now that it was a way adults could show both approval and disbelief at the same moment. Maybe they were just being noncommittal, maybe they were suspending disbelief, but I think it is a healthy reply to make to a child. After having meandered through some probably awkward and highly improbable description of events, half concocted, half actual, it is much better to hear an adult say "Imagine that!" then to have him tell you you're a liar, stupid or otherwise at fault. Better than having some patient parental unit of the present day try to be helpful about the difference between reality and fantasy. "Imagine that" had many tones and shades of meaning, from true amazement with a real exclamation mark to a slightly ironic twist with disbelief just below the surface. But whatever its tone, it always gives you the benefit of the doubt, allows your version of things to stand.

Taking Kathleen and Harold around the Avalon Peninsula left me in a continuous "imagine that" condition. Since I am the product of a late-twentieth-century, pseudo-socialist, historically conscious, ecologically sensitive ideology, the idea that one would want to tour anything except natural or historic sites dumbfounds me. On the other hand, my parents, unrepentant admirers of technological "progress," wanted us to go to see the building of the deep-sea oil rigs at Bull Arm. Dad had been there before, so he was doing this for our benefit. We were reluctant; he was insistent. And I ended up enjoying the tour. Imagine that. I think he took me there to be impressed with the giant concrete circle being built in the middle of the Bay, and the enormous dockside complex that would eventually sit atop the circle when it is finally anchored out at sea. And I have to admit, at an intellectual level it is an impressive idea, that humans can make such an artificial island, and that if we are really lucky, and our science is right, it will survive the North Atlantic. What impressed me most was the enormity of the human effort that made it possible. One of my Newfoundland cousins had gone all the way to Korea to help supervise the installation of the electrical systems in one of the pods that will be at the top of the artificial island. And his expertise was only one of thousands needed to make this project happen. The young woman who guided us as we toured the site in a school bus recited the statistics of how many people are fed each day, how many eggs must be cracked, potatoes peeled, steaks grilled and fish fried, described the lock-step system of supplying, servicing and supervising that must go on when the crews are working three shifts a day during the "continuous pour" of concrete that makes the giant circle possible. She was quick with accurate statistics when I asked how many women and in what capacities were employed on the site. I'll have you know that this Newfoundland project has managed to employ more women directly in the technological and building side of this project than just about anywhere. I forget the statistic, but I was impressed at the time. "Imagine that," I thought.

As we walked up the stairs to the viewing site to see the giant grey structure circled by the bright blue water, I thought of the graveyard at Julie's Cove and all the ways Newfoundlanders have had to reinvent themselves to make a living on their island. Our guide described the new techniques that have made it possible to keep work on the project going nine months a year, through fog, storm and all but the coldest winter days. It sounded difficult; it sounded dangerous. I remembered a story from one of my school readers about a boy from a tiny outport who—on an everyday journey from one place to another—took terrible risks with sea and fog. I especially remembered the low-key reaction of everyone, including himself, when he managed to come safely to land. Despite our guide's sureness about the way the project has improved upon already-sophisticated Scandinavian technology, and her careful explanation of the stress tests the models of the rig have undergone that show it will resist all that nature can hand out—all perhaps except an earthquake under the sea—I had my doubts. Newfoundlanders would still be taking risks with sea and fog. "Imagine that," I said carefully in response to our guide's articulate enthusiasm.

Another day, attempting to wean my parents from their preference for sites of Newfoundland progress and industry, I convinced them to come to the archeological digs at Ferryland, where Memorial University is unearthing several layers of habitation that help them reconstruct settlement of that part of the island, the earliest (except for the brief Norse visit) white settlement in North America. We dropped Richard at Witless Bay from where he would go on a boat ride to photograph sea birds—puffins, murres and kittiwakes. My parents said they had seen enough birds in their day so they and I headed on to the digs. The university people have the site nicely laid out so that you can observe the various processes of an archeological dig safely at the same time as the workers and students continue their painstaking exploration. Once again, a well-informed young woman guided us. My parents have a tendency to distract such guides by trying to guess which part of Newfoundland they come from. This is not easy, since young people in Newfoundland today often have only trace remains of their local accents. My parents are persistent and quite good at this guessing game, and the guides are patient, perhaps understanding the dislike my parents' generation have for depersonalized guided tours. Kathleen and Harold, quite insistently, work to establish a more personal relationship, asking biographical questions, offering up their own backgrounds in return. This young guide seemed determined to tell us something about the site and even though my father interrupted to correct her history a couple of times, she did manage to do quite a good job of our education. However, somewhere between showing us the well that was built by the first white inhabitants and explaining the way the workers had laid out the vegetable garden to imitate the first one on this spot, Dad and I noticed that Mother was missing.

After a brief flurry of excitement we found Kathleen, being escorted carefully, and very slowly, out of the forbidden-to-the-public depths of one of the digs, while she questioned her young male companion for details of his place of origin and his parents background. Father questioned her in turn: "How did you get down there, Kathleen?" To this she replied, "How do you think? I walked, of course!"

I scolded her: "But you're not supposed. . . ." She interrupted me with a haughty, "There's nothing wrong with asking a boy where his people are from." This desire to locate origins made me remember the typical question asked by adults who did not know me on my childhood visits to my mother's birthplace in Carbonear. They did not ask "Who are you?" but "Whose child are you, my maid?" I learned to say, "I'm Mom Osmond's granddaughter, Mrs. Arthur Osmond that is. I'm her girl Kathleen's child." And to those who further inquired, "and who would your father be, then?" I would reply, "Harold Clarke, from Victoria village, who was Aunt Ann's son who used to live up in the 'Burnt Woods.'" These were correct answers to questions of identity in those days.

On the way back to Witless Bay to pick up Richard, mother regaled us with all that she had learned down in the digs. Some of it was even about archeology. Imagine that. When his boat docked Richard was ecstatic over the sea birds and whales he had seen. He leaned in the car window, tried to persuade us to take the next trip by telling us how the whales had come right up to the boat, followed them, churning and surfacing and singing beside them. Aboard the boat the captain's son had sung sea shanties and finally all the mammals, those aboard the boat and those in the water were inspired to sing together. Kathleen and Harold were polite during this recitation; they had seen many whales in their lifetimes, sung many a sea shanty, knew the difference between a whale and a whale of a story. "Imagine that," they commented politely.

Our best day was full of sunshine on a blue-green ocean, perfect for a visit to the birthplaces of my parents on Conception Bay. But the trip did not start out easy. On each of our day trips I would haul out the map of the Avalon Peninsula, preparing to act as navigator from behind as Richard drove (it's strictly men in the front, women in the back with Kathleen and Harold on board). Each day my parents would insist that I put the map away. "We know exactly where we are going," they would exclaim. Miles later on there would be mild doubts: "We should have come to that turnoff by now." Or, "this corner is all changed." I took to memorizing the route on the map before they woke up in the morning, and then whispering it into Richard's left ear from my place behind him in the back seat. But my parents voices, both absolutely convinced of their own routes (which were often different) would assail him from his right and right rear. This particular morning Richard tried to call above our voices that he could hear no one. (My husband does not shout; he is from the Prairies and the strong, silent school of manhood). We all continued giving directions. Finally, observing that Richard was becoming quite disoriented, I had to shout them down. So that my mother would not take my edict personally, and, so as not to be seen to favour myself, I made the rule that no one in the back seat could give any directions. This put the burden of navigation firmly on my father, and I insisted that he take the map. In fact, I threw it over the seat at him. He took it in hand, carefully displaying his ability to compromise, and never once opened it on the rest of our journey. We found our way to the town of Victoria, to Salmon Cove and Crocker's Cove and on to the regional centre at Carbonear despite the fact that father generally did not tell Richard where to turn until we were on the wrong road. Then he would ask with the wonder of a man who knew his way home blindfolded, "How come you didn't take the road to Victoria back there?" After turning the car around in several driveways, Richard finally learned to ask "which way?" at every intersection.

Carbonear, Victoria, Salmon Cove and Crocker's Cove. The circle of these four places loop the memories of my parents' childhood and youth as well as the history of my family and its four centuries in this place. As we approached the road to the "Burnt Woods," Harold's birthplace, my father warned me that we would probably not be able to get very far on it. He had been here a few years back with my brother Peter and they had not made it all the way up the Church Road to the old homestead. This was all the challenge I needed. I would go where no brother had gone before. Despite the fact that the road quickly became as rough as an old river bottom, I managed to get the car all the way to a small bridge that my parents assured me was only a short walk from our destination. We walked on and quickly found the only remains of my grandmother's house, a small grassy field and the foundation stones of a root cellar. We picnicked on the stones as Richard took photographs and Kathleen told us of how, as a young woman, she would come from Carbonear to visit her cousins in Victoria and walk with them up this road in the evening in the hopes of meeting Harold.

As she talked, my father left us, heading up the slight incline of the former road. I did not expect him to go far; we had already tired him with the walk from the car and our explorations toward the stream that bordered the property. After a little while, when he failed to return, I joked to my mother that maybe the fairies had taken him. Her face smiled, but her eyes held another less confident look. I had a sudden panic about an old man of eighty-five, who only a few years ago had had heart bypass surgery and even now only barely controlled his tricky heart with a pacemaker and medication. What was I thinking of, allowing him to go off by himself? What would my brothers and sister say if I lost him in his birthplace?

It must have been a good half kilometre before I caught him. He was striding with considerable energy toward the horizon. I remembered being told by my Uncle Rich of my grandmother heading off into the woods, her head captured by the fairies; I remembered my own daughter's tendency, as a small child, to keep walking briskly in a straight line toward the horizon whenever I let her out of my arms and I thought of the way I tend to lose my consciousness in walking and end up miles from where I intended to be. I had to call to him to make him stop. When I told him I was afraid because of the story of grandmother and the fairies he laughed and explained to me the history of the forest around us; how it had been burned before settlement (thus its name), had grown back into a thick rich forest by his youth, and now could only manage the small scattered growth we saw around us because of all the woodcutting that had gone on since his time here. He told me about the other homes that had been along the road, about his brother Rich coming up here to look for the horse that had strayed, about the berry picking and the vegetable garden and the swimming in the creek long, long ago.

By the time we returned to our picnic spot he was eighty-five again and very tired. I hiked down to where we left the car, examining the ruts of the road as I went to see how I might avoid scraping the car bottom, and with considerable care and caution, managed to bring the vehicle to where he was. By then a man with a fishing pole had walked out of the woods and father and mother were busy acquiring his history. He was a Clarke of a different family, and although friendly he seemed unimpressed by the fact that my parents knew his grandfather, as later the young university student mowing the grass in the cemetery would not be surprised that our name was Clarke like hers; the graveyard was full of them.

In Salmon Cove we had a hard time finding the place where my Aunt Susie, father's sister, had lived with Uncle John all those years of her married life. Mother went into the post office where they remembered Susie and pointed to the spot. By then we had had a whole morning of finding traces of houses and graves, and my parents were tired, but agreed that we could go to see the Sands at Salmon Cove, since I remembered it as the most beautiful ocean spot of my childhood. Its grey-black sands were still stunning and the larger world has now realized this beauty for it has been made into a nature reserve. Richard and I walked the strand of beach in silence, except for my announcement of the next stage of the day. I intended to head back to St. John's by the fastest route since my parents seemed so tired.

I had underestimated the energizing power of remembering. When we returned to our car they were all enthusiasm again, explaining how we must go back to Carbonear by the Crocker's Cove route so we could see the land our ancestors settled in the first years of the 1600s. On the way, they both kept up a running commentary of their youthful exploits as each hill and dale brought new memories. At the sight of Carbonear Island we were told the story of mother's teaching days in Crocker's Cove, when she took the students to Carbonear Island to relive their ancestors' defence against the French invaders, and we heard father's recitation of the battles between the Newfoundlanders and the French. I had heard these stories often before and had regretted their anti-French subtext, but here, in this treeless, exposed ocean place, they began to make sense. Given the unprotected nature of this landscape our ancestors must certainly have been the underdogs. Suddenly, my father commanded Richard to stop the car. "Here it is; here it is, the ancestral home!" Ahead of me, glimpsed between the shoulders of my husband and my father, jutting narrowly into the ocean, was a small rocky peninsula with grass enough for maybe a goat. None of the trees and brooks of Victoria village, none of the town life of Carbonear, no sandy strand to walk on. This was certainly the most disadvantaged place we had seen that day. The rocks descended steeply from their small grassy tops to the ocean below. How could they have lived here, in this treeless place unprotected against the wind coming off the ocean on three sides?

"Father, you could hardly cultivate a cabbage on that land." My parents laughed. "Fish, my dear, fish. They cultivated fish flakes."

I pictured the various houses that must have been raised on that barren ground over the years since 1600, from the sod huts of the dangerous times of early settlement to the salt-box style, two-storey wooden houses of my great-grandparents' era. I pictured a house surrounded by fish flakes. The small sheltered place where the grass grew greener must have been where the cabbages were planted. I pictured those hundreds of years of bloodlines, the fishermen, the sailors and the working (always working) women going on in this place generation after generation. All of their energy and toughness, all of their foolishness and failure, all of their hearts' blood, pounding away inside me. Imagine that.

The place gave Harold and Kathleen even more energy. For the rest of the day they traipsed their tired juniors around the whole of Conception Bay: a visit to mother's family graveyard, a chat with a very much alive Aunt Ann, my mother's sister-in-law, a drink with old friends of my parents. By the end of the day, driving back into St. John's, I felt as if I had lived all my life in my parents' memories, not my own. St. John's, my own childhood place, felt unreal again. I felt unattached, floating in a dream of white grave markers against craggy rock shimmering on an ocean of bright turquoise memory. I needed to see things separate from my parents; I needed to do it alone.

But there seemed no moment, in the few days left of our visit, to be alone. We drove my parents to see old friends and relatives, and at sunset we went to Signal Hill to watch the sun set over the city and the lights gradually come on until St. John's became a necklace of light glittering in its reflective harbour. Another day we met Eleanor and her mother for lunch, while the men went on a tour of Ron's workplace, the science and engineering centres at the university. Another day, Dad insisted that we see the Newfoundland Maritime Museum and since we happened to be in St. John's on the day the "tall ships" were arriving Richard and I joined the crowds on the South Side, facing the crowds across the harbour, at the Battery and Signal Hill, to cheer the sailed vessels as they navigated the narrows.

This last event reminded me that I had never been to Fort Amherst, the rocky promontory that is at the end of the South Side Road. My father assured me there was not much to see, since no restoration had taken place, but to humour me they went along on our last evening. There is no place to park at the end of the South Side Road, so my parents stayed with the car after Richard convinced a local resident to let him park his elderly in-laws and his car in the man's parking space. Richard and I went to explore the old lighthouse and the rocks that met the Atlantic over the low red granite of the cliffs. I lost Richard at one point. He told me later he had found a ledge of rock where some young women were sharing a case of beer, and he had asked if he could take their photograph. They had agreed, laughing, asking him if it would be used by the police to arrest them for their illegal activity.

So I walked back to the car without him, and managed a few minutes of being alone. If you walk back from Fort Amherst at sunset, you see a different view from the panorama that takes your breath away on Signal Hill. This is no tourist photo opportunity to be captured with one perfect picture which you can blow up into a poster and say to your friends, "Now, here, see, isn't my homeland beautiful?" To walk back from the low cliffs of Fort Amherst is to see the city as a moving picture. At first it is hidden from you, only the deep trench of the narrows and the cliffs of Signal Hill beyond can be seen. Then the city comes into view, not from the lofty height of the hill, but at eye-level across the harbour so that you see the daily workplace of the waterfront against the impossible steepness of the streets that tail up from it towards the upper town. To see the city from this place, from where I had never seen it, made me sit down on the rocks to take it in, street by street, building by building. It was as if my own childhood were over there, on the north side among those buildings. It was as if I, on the south side of the harbour, were separated, not by time but only by space, from a place where I still belonged. I tried to imagine what kind of woman I would have become if I had not left that place when I was a month short of fourteen. I pulled my knees up to rest my chin and meditated for some time, watching the city move from daylight to darkness. But I could not imagine that, could not imagine the Newfoundland woman I might have become; I was from away, and even if away had become only a harbour's width it could not be spanned by my imagination.

As I returned down the narrow road, the sounds from the homes built against the cliffs of the South Side Hill seemed magnified. People's voices, the sounds of dishes being washed, music playing, television, all the ordinary sounds of a summer evening were intensely alive, intensely real. I was away from them and I understood that being from away helped me hear them with the keenness of those who cannot come home.

Each time I have left Newfoundland in past years it has been in conditions of stress, with a profound sense of being glad to get away safely. My parents tell me that when I was a baby and we moved to Nova Scotia during the war, the ferry was darkened for fear of submarine attack. When I was a teenager and our family left for the West, we rushed to our airplane during a break in days of late winter fog. I was ecstatic that the long overdue flight was actually taking off. As I watched my mother shed tears for leaving her home behind I could hardly wait to discover the prairie city that was our destination. Returning from our camper trip in the sixties with our young children, Richard and I met gale force winds heading back down the west coast to cross on the ferry at Port aux Basques. The chains that held our camper to the truck tugged and jerked, groaning with the effort of hanging on. A few years back, on our last visit, we took off during a May rain-squall and the plane bounced its way to sunshine at 30,000 feet. Looking down through the breaks in the clouds I could see icebergs, formidably close to the coastline.

This time we set out from Placentia, choosing the fourteen-hour ferry ride to North Sydney rather than the long drive to the west coast of the island to catch the Port aux Basques ferry. Being notorious for motion sickness as a child, I had worried about so many hours on the water. But the day was a gift of sunshine, warm winds and an ocean as smooth as the proverbial glass of that worn image. I sat on deck most of the day, watching the shore recede, caught by the play of light on water, hypnotized by the wind around me, the parting of the waters ahead of me. Newfoundland had given me a "sun rays crowned her golden hills, and summer spreads her hand," kind of day, just like the old anthem I sang as a girl promised me in those days before I became a Canadian. It was a gentle leave-taking, one that made me want to come again; one that invited me to realize why I had come back to this place. I had been writing memoir stories for a few years now, starting them on my study leave in Florida when a more southern ocean had lulled me into memory. I had revised them, rethought them, tinkered with them for years, in all sorts of places from Victoria to Halifax. At this moment, in the wind of the ferry deck with the island of my girlhood slipping behind me, I wanted more than anything to return to those stories and make them ready for you. Imagine that.

War: Mother's Child

*T*he sight and sound of a toilet flushing might be the first memory of anyone born and raised in the privileged part of the world in the twentieth century: a first memory made from machinery and technology. This is not a very promising start if I wanted an image for an archetypal childhood journey into nostalgia. I might prefer an origin moment like that of a woman from the !Kung tribe in Africa, whose life story I once read. She was able to tell in detail a childhood quite different from mine. She told of her weaning from her mother, how she loved the comfort of the exclusive use of her mother's breasts, until a new child was due and it was time to stop, how she yearned and cried and fought and finally hated the new brother, wanting him dead, until her dad and mom reasoned and shamed her out of it. She was well along in years, maybe four or more before all this happened. Now there's a portentous way to begin a life! On the other hand, I think I must have been aged two, long weaned from my bottle and assumed to be a very grown up little thing, by the time I became frightened of toilets flushing. But I am getting ahead of myself. Let me start at the beginning where a good story should.

When I was thirty-eight years old I had accomplished the nifty late-twentieth-century act of balancing a marriage, three children, and a career and was—as any woman who has done this will tell you—a little out of breath and in danger of losing my balance. So, like a good girl of my times I went to a psychiatrist to get balanced again. I like to get things done fast and I thought therapy should work something like getting a wheel-balance job done to make the car run smoothly again. I was surprised when it lasted a year. Looking back, I accomplished a lot in that year: remembered significant events of childhood, began to

understand my need to sometimes behave like an infant in my significant relationships, found an antidepressant medication that held my
balancing act balanced and tentatively started to work at not blaming
my mother for my life.

In therapy I had explosive visual dream images of what might be
called the pre-memory years, one in which a terrified little girl is left in
a crib so long that cobwebs grow over her. This dream came very early
in the first weeks of therapy and in many ways rhythmed that first year,
since my feelings for that dream-child were intense and painful. We
talked a lot about that dream, my therapist and I, never finding a memory that went with it. Instead, I found strength from the exploration to
go on with my life. I discontinued my sessions after one year, not wanting to become like those movie stars who cling for decades to their
shrinks' hands. Midway through the next year I had another dream that
propelled me back to the therapist's office for what I now like to call the
real work. One morning, at a time when I had become convinced that I
was "cured"—and wasn't I a bright girl to have done it in only a year—I
woke smiling as a dream replayed itself instantly. I was in my therapist's office, which in my dream was filled with lush plants and flowers,
and I was looking for something. I peeked under each spreading
branch, excusing myself politely when I had to disturb the secretary at
her desk in order to check under the philodendron leaves. Finally, off in
a corner, I saw a small child, tucked away beside some ferns, curled in a
tight fetal knot. I picked her up like the infinitely precious treasure I
now know her to be, and carried her to my therapist. "Here she is." I
said, "I've found her." We both smiled as the child slept on. This dream
was so pure in its direction to me that as soon as I got out of bed, I
called my ex-therapist and in a kind of crazed glee made an appoint-
ment to start again. And thus began the time spent waking up the child
that I offer you now. So here she is.

But I can't give her to you so simply. Writing doesn't work like
that. Life doesn't work like that. At the moment I typed the line, "Here
she is," the phone rang. It was my baby brother Peter, phoning from
Nova Scotia. He is now in his forties; I have a decade on him and I am
definitely his "older sister." When he was a child of four I terrorized
him. One weekend when I was just fourteen and my brother David was
seventeen we were left with the younger children while our parents
went on a business convention. Dave came home occasionally from
hanging out with his friends to check things out, but there was no doubt

in either of our minds who was in charge of food and care. My mother had told me to make sure little Peter ate a good breakfast, especially his egg, as he was too thin, ate badly and it was her constant aim to supplement the french fries, orange juice, and white bread topped with mayonnaise diet that was his preference, with the protein of eggs. Of course he would not eat his egg for a mere teenaged sister and I chased him all over the house until he finally hid screaming in a closet, begging me not to hit him. Did I hit him? I must ask him sometime.

I did not ask this morning when he phoned. We talked about what we both agree on, the absolute wonderfulness of his daughter Maggie. She is named after me, after my writing name actually. She is the real Margaret Clarke and her father and I agree that she and her every act are noteworthy. When my baby brother called his daughter after me, Richard said I was "tickled." "You won't admit it will you, but you are just plain tickled," said he, and I was. What an odd word "tickled," one neither he nor I ever use. But I was exactly that: "tickled." The thought of her always brings me unconditional pleasure, the kind no child of your own can ever give, because the responsibility prevents pure pleasure. But when I think of the real Margaret Clarke, I have the pleasure of a good tickle.

Inventing your writing self by the act of rescuing your middle and maiden names can have some surprising results. I have recently discovered that another niece of mine, Margo, has the name Margaret Clarke on her birth certificate. She was not called after my writing name, since when she was born, I had not written. Her mother suggested to me that in a sense I had taken up her daughter's name for my books. She was smiling at the time so I assume that my use of the name is acceptable.

What I meant to say, before naming conveniently distracted me from the guilt of my attack on my four-year-old brother, was that the thought of hitting a child always sets off a physical reaction in me that is quite the opposite of tickling: that feeling of pure fear you have when you find that inside you is a terrible violence, a violence which if ever unleashed will devastate the bodies of those you love. That was what sent me to a psychiatrist in the first place: the terror almost got out. Despite my policy of no corporal punishment of children, I hit my ten-year-old daughter. Once. Hard. Across the front of her body. I screamed at her that her tears were driving me crazy. Even writing this brings a tension across my chest and a grief so huge, for the children I have terrorized with my terror, that it is hard to write. I will stop until I can find a way to tell you about that child I found under the greenery of my dream.

It is harder to do this than I imagined. Real people keep getting in the way. Between this paragraph and the last, between yesterday and today I have heard from two of my three children, both of whom are at points of change in their adult lives. As I did my laps in the pool this morning it was hard to drive their lives from my head, hard not to be the mother, to use up my writing energy in creating fantasies for my children's lives. It is hard to free myself from motherhood and tell the story of that sleeping child. Hard also, because yesterday my mother phoned. She is so real. It is hard to take her out of her eighty-year-old reality, the tough lady who has more psychic energy than several of her children and grandchildren combined, hard to make her into the young Kathleen that I need for my story. Writing memoir is hard too; it keeps wanting to be fiction, it keeps wanting to be history. It is hard to stay on the line between history and fiction in order to make a life.

My mother was one of six sisters. There were two brothers, but that is not nearly as important as the fact of having five sisters. Whenever she did something as a young girl, if she needed company, there was always a sister. If she needed to go to a dance or a movie, or just walk down the "Back Lane" of Carbonear, Newfoundland, there was always a sister. If Kathleen sometimes felt overwhelmed with sisters, well, that was part of being home, being safe. If she needed advice on hairstyle or dresses, there was her older sister Helen, who was generous, capable and knew the larger world of the city. Kathleen boarded with Helen when she came from the family home in Carbonear to the city of St. John's. My mother was the "smart one" in the family and went to teachers' college. No one else in her family had ever done that.

My mother's family were not what you would call poor Newfoundlanders, since they managed to stay off the "dole" in the "dirty thirties," a canny accomplishment for any family from Conception Bay who depended on the itinerant work of a breadwinner who was trained to be a sailing captain in an age when sail had disappeared. My grandfather slipped on a log while building a dock, broke his back and died. My grandmother supported the family as a midwife after that. Kathleen managed to go to teachers' training with the help of scholarships, Helen's care and a gift of money from her older brother. It was quite an accomplishment. Despite the fact that she did very well in college they didn't offer her the position at the school in Carbonear which she applied for, since it had to be saved for a girl with an influential father. But they did give her a school a few miles down the road, at Crocker's Cove, the home of many of her ancestors and of my father's too. Mother says that the older boys in her one-room school wore hobnailed boots which they sometimes managed to connect with her thin, sensitive legs as she bent to help them with their desk work.

My mother was the first teacher in Crocker's Cove to take the children on what we now call a field trip. She hired a man to row her whole gang of kids, ages six to sixteen to Carbonear Island in his dory and there she told her students how their ancestors had held out against the French in 1696, while towns all around the Avalon were pillaged and burned, while families from Portugal Cove and Holyrood to Harbour Main and Port de Grave fled before the French. But the ancestors of these students, their very own able-bodied ancestors, men and women alike, having moved their helpless ones—from the eldest infirm old lady down to the smallest child—into the woods of the valley road, armed themselves and rowed out to Carbonear Island to resist the invaders' several attacks. The French finally gave up trying to kill the people of Carbonear, Crocker's Cove and Harbour Grace and left. In 1705 the settlers had to do it all over again, since their neglectful English masters had made it obvious to the French that this particular part of the growing British Empire was easy pickings.

Those were the days when the life of a year-round resident in Newfoundland was worth less than nothing to the folks who ran things back at the centre of Empire. My people began as a forbidden people, forbidden to live on the very soil they knew as home. They had been on "the Rock" since the early 1600s, but were not allowed to hold land titles until the next century. They were worth less than slaves to the home-country merchants who wished to be rid of them, since they could not sell a white man that they didn't want. I tell you these details so that you will know that my mother is no clinging vine, that she and her kind are smart; they have survival skills and imagination. But the company of sisters was also important.

When my maternal grandmother, Olivia Osmond, was told that Kathleen wanted to marry Harold Clarke she is supposed to have commented that she thought Kathleen was too foolish to marry, but since Harold Clarke had sense enough for two, she was not overly concerned. Marry they did and two years later had my brother, whose first name is Samuel, but who has always been called by his second name, David, and three years after that they had me, whose first name is Helen, and is not called by her second name, Margaret. My dad says that my birth cry was a scream of absolute anger. The story of my absolute anger at birth has become a family joke. My brothers have been known to elaborate on the birth story, honing the figure of anger into a lifetime of inappropriate behaviour. But that's another story. When you dig behind the anger at birth as metaphor, there is a history. There is always a history. You just have to find it and shape it to your needs.

It seems that at the beginning of her ninth month of pregnancy my mother wanted to borrow something from the next-door neighbour who had a very vicious dog. I would like to tell you she was trying to borrow a gravy boat or a fruit bowl or some other grail-like object, suitable to a birth story, but I am afraid I cannot tell you the exact goal of her mission. Anyway, she approached the yard and yes, there was the dog, full of teeth and growling. Kathleen was certain that she could just make it to the neighbour's door before the dog got her, and she really did need whatever it was she wanted to borrow. Halfway up the pathway she saw that her certainty was mistaken and the dog was going to get her if she didn't change her plans quickly. She leapt for the fence and hurdled it, feeling the painful pull of tearing in her eight-month pregnant belly as she did so. She went home and cried. Her water broke that night and I came angrily into the world the next afternoon at six o'clock, one month early, and have continued to be pretty angry, by all accounts, for a number of decades. I have always made it a point to avoid dogs. As a child I would go blocks out of my way to do so. After I had therapy I learned to stare dogs down, but I still don't like them and neither does Kathleen.

Just recently my mother told me another version of this story. In it she is not off on any borrowing adventures, does not jump any fences. She is hanging out clothes in her own backyard and the neighbour calls her to the fence to talk. She is terribly afraid of the wolf-like dog, but the neighbour says not to worry, he's harmless. The dog jumps the fence, leaps up my mother's body to her throat, the neighbour still insisting on her doggie's good nature. Kathleen is so traumatized she gives birth the next day. I don't like this second story, preferring mother the guilty but self-empowered risk-taker to mother the innocent victim. I'm almost certain that years ago she used to tell the other version. Surely I have not imagined this. I have noticed that since I've become a writer Kathleen is more careful with her stories. I don't want to lie to you so I let you make what you will of both versions.

One fact I can be sure of is that the day I was born was March 28, 1941. I found my original birth certificate this very morning as I checked my childhood history book, *The Story of Newfoundland*, seeking to find what my mother might have told those children on Carbonear Island that had anything to do with the stories we call history. However, no history book will tell you why March 28, 1941 is an important date for me and lots of other women. I'm sure there are all sorts of things that were happening that day and an encyclopedia yearbook will tell you about them if you want to look. But it will not tell you what I am about to tell you. To know the importance of March 28, 1941, you have to have lived a woman's life in the latter days of capitalism in the West, learned its workloads for middle-class females, the compromises it enforces, the betrayals it encourages and the smallness of the rebellions that class privilege makes possible, learned them with such sureness that you pretty well break under the load. Then you have to make your damaged self well enough to learn how to study. Harder still, you have to disobey the rules when you study, seeking illogical adjacencies, remote occurrences and unlikely contingencies that are considered of no relevance whatsoever to whatever your subject of study is.

That's what I did. One day when I was forty and working as a graduate student in a university library on an annotated bibliography of the works by and about a famous male poet, a class assignment which needed to be done right there and then, I left my assignment to wander the library bookshelves and find a reason to be distracted. I did. I found Virginia Woolf. Years earlier, when I was an undergraduate in the late fifties and early sixties we had studied Joyce and Eliot until we thought Modernists were the only thing that mattered in literature, outside of Shakespeare. But at that time Virginia was mentioned only occasionally, as a sort of writer manqué, a talented woman who just didn't quite make the Eliot/Joyce-defined grade, like people such as Elizabeth Barrett Browning and Emily Dickinson. Later, when I returned after a career as a high school teacher to do graduate work, I discovered Woolf had become fashionable in feminist circles, so I read her works on my own. But I had never read about her life.

On this occasion, looking for an excuse to further delay working on my assignment, I took a book off the shelf that gave a brief biography of Woolf. There, right in the chronology of her life, was the important fact that nobody had told me. At eleven o'clock on the morning of March 28, 1941, Virginia stuffed rocks in her pockets and walked into the River

Ouse and drowned. I didn't find out about the rocks until years later, but I like the detail. If you are going to do it, do it right and let them know you did it, that it was no silly slip of the foot, fainting in madness or heartbreak, no Ophelia or Lady of Shalott, bleating when they should have tried swimming.

I have calculated the time differential between England and Newfoundland, and reckon that it was around dawn of March 28, 1941, just when Kathleen must have been getting really scared that this baby was going to come too early for its own good, that Virginia did it. I want you to know that my ego is not so inflated that I believe that all of Virginia's spirit rushed across the Atlantic, and like some jet-stream incubus flew up my mother's vagina and into the little baby vagina of yours truly. There was too much of Virginia for that. It may have taken months, years, for all the energy in Virginia to get properly accommodated in various little girl bodies around the globe. It may have taken a thousand little girl babies, maybe a million, to use up the suppressed anger that a life like hers must have gathered. I meet these little girls every now and then, all aging now. They pass me in hallways, in stairwells, in streets; we make eye contact, but do not speak. We are a generation trained to keep quiet about what we really think, but our eyes tell each other that we serve the same lady.

I like to think that there in Britain's oldest colony my mother's distress went out like Marconi's first wireless message, shooting out from Signal Hill into the ether of the universe. I like to believe it was picked up loud and clear by some part of the energy that Virginia never got to use, and one small distilled drop of her most suppressed anger—maybe the part that could never admit it hated doctors who shut her up in dark rooms and forbade her books; maybe the part that didn't like to admit that Leonard was not God's gift of a perfect husband to a female writer; maybe the part that wished her mother had loved her more than that demanding old man, her father. Some tiny pearl of anger, pressed as tight as matter in a dark hole in the universe—I like to think I got that bit.

After I wrote that part about Virginia yesterday morning I had a hard day. Having a hard day doesn't keep me from doing the work I've brought with me on my study leave. Like the obedient scholar/editor I am I spent the day reading other people's autobiographical manuscripts, making difficult decisions about which twenty of fifty-five I can choose for publication in the special issue I am editing for a literary journal. (I have already sent back nearly three hundred from writers who have things to say that are at least as important as what I am writing now.) Through the day of reading manuscripts, through the late afternoon walk along Sand Key beach, through the two scotches and the dependably beautiful sunset of this Florida ocean place, through my husband Richard's good cooking, I kept whipping myself about that word "anger." I was so guilty about the anger that late in the evening I stuffed my face with food I did not need.

You see, I've been planning that Virginia part in my head for years now, tasting it privately for its sweetness, before I set it down on paper to make it real. There was never anything about anger in it. Not ever. It was about energy, the energy of a writing life. The anger comes as soon as my writing begins. It must be Virginia's anger. It is certainly not mine. My life is not one to be angry about. Now if I had hidden in some cellar in Nazi Europe, and by some miracle survived to find my people dead, then I could have anger. If my mama had washed white people's toilets in Mississippi and then had to sit at the back of some bus she had damn well paid to ride, then I would deserve my anger. If I had walked out of Hiroshima a naked child with leukemia in my every cell, enough to deform generations after me, then I would have earned anger. But I have not earned anger, not even Virginia's. I should be writing about little Helen with a touch of tender nostalgia, perhaps the occasional sad regret, but merging always with the pleasure of having grown up in a lucky place, a lucky family.

Let me try again.

When I was one month old, Kathleen and Harold had to leave Newfoundland. My father's wartime job as a translator and censor of international cable communication was to take him to North Sydney in Nova Scotia where the continental cable came ashore. Mother says I was not a happy baby, cried much of the time, but as soon as the train moved I slept. Of course, as soon as it stopped I screamed. The "Newfie Bullet" stopped often. Aboard the ferry I was blessedly lulled to sleep by the heartbeat of the engines and the fact that the whole ship was in blackout, creeping its wartime pace across the long hours to Nova Scotia. I was surprised to discover recently that North Sydney, where the ferry from Newfoundland docks, is not a bad little town. Driving through its quiet treed streets told me nothing of my early memory of it as a great darkness: little foggy halos of light with darkness pressing close upon my family and me.

I realize now that I don't really have any proper memories of those three years spent in North Sydney, but I have absorbed Kathleen's. I discovered this when I finally got around to questioning my mother in a professional way about those years. By professional I mean I am a teacher and I have decades of experience in getting answers out of people who do not think they have much to say on a subject, or that what they have to say has already been said, or perhaps shouldn't be said. It's a neat ability, sort of like being a therapist, except they pay you less.

My mother told me the usual stories she had always told about North Sydney: "One winter day you and David went sledding and I'll never forget when he brought you home. I couldn't see your face for blood. And the screeching; the screeching! You had slid right into the corner of a house, hitting it with your forehead. I had no one of my own in North Sydney, you know. So I threw on my coat and rushed you off to this doctor I'd never even met. He was a mean one, that one. I was holding you in my arms and you were thrashing and screaming. He just leaned over and took the two pieces of skin gapping on your forehead and pinched them shut, pinched them shut just like this (she demonstrates). You fainted and I almost did too, but I was holding you, so I couldn't. He sewed you up while you were out." I rub the scar in the middle of my forehead and smile. We all know the story's truth, for here it is, written on my skin.

Another story that we have all heard a hundred times is the story about the day my father left for officers' training in the Canadian armed forces. I am supposed to have stood at the kitchen window, in high wail, chanting over and over again: "My daddy gone, neber took me." When mother tells the story she imitates the grammar and pronunciation, as well as the hysteria and grief of the child's voice: "My Daddy gone, neber took me." According to her I went on for hours. Usually when mother tells this story, we all nod and someone remarks on what a difficult child Helen was, and mother rushes on to another Helen story.

"Do you know what she did when her father came home in his officer's uniform? He was so proud, you know, so proud of that uniform. And he did look good, I'll give him that. He looked handsome. He told me to dress Helen up and he'd take her for a walk in the park. Helen was his favourite, you know. He just thought the world of Helen. So I dressed her all up and put her bonnet on to cover the fact that her hair was as straight as a poker. How I used to work at that skimpy bit of hair! She always had such thin hair. I'd work, trying to get some curl in

it and she would cry and pull away. So I just gave up and I would curl
the front a little bit and then clamp the bonnet on. Remember, Helen,
the verse we used to say? 'There was a little girl, who had a little curl,
right in the middle of her forehead, and when she was good, she was
very very good, and when she was bad she was horrid.' Anyway, I put
her bonnet on and off they went. Pretty soon I see him rushing back
and Helen screaming. Do you know what she did? She peed all over his
army uniform."

Mother laughs in delight at this point, or sometimes for father's
sake she takes a tone of pretended shock. "He was mad as anything,
and mad at Helen too. There he was, in his brand new army uniform
and she peed all over the front. I had such a time getting the smell out.
I'm sure it was still there when he went back to Ontario."

These stories are part of a parcel that make our family a family.
Mother has other stories that highlight her other four children, and usually tells the appropriate stories to the appropriate child and/or grandchild. I think that these stories once were the way Newfoundlanders
made a history of their own. Everyone in Newfoundland used to tell stories. Many still do. When I finally questioned my mother rigorously
about my early years—I was in the middle of therapy then and there is
nothing more ruthless than the desire to know of a forty-year-old
woman in therapy—I discovered why that scary darkness surrounds all
my feelings about those early times. My mother started to tell the
usual stories, but I now noticed—because of my new found therapy
alertness—that at the moment of crisis in all her stories she always
spoke the same words: "I had no one of my own in North Sydney, you
know." This time I broke into her narrative.

"That must have been hard for you," I said, imitating the understatement of my quiet-voiced therapist. Instantly, her tears came, and
they kept coming. We were sitting on the balcony of this apartment,
here beside the Gulf of Mexico, the very place I write in today. I got up
fast and closed the glass door to the living room, so my father would not
hear and ask in that rather annoyed, but fearful voice: "Kathleen, what
are you crying about, what on earth have you got to cry about." To
father's mind, given the success he has had in life and the generous way
he has supplied his wife with every comfort he could afford, including a
condo in Florida, mother's tears are illogical. With the door shut on the
rationality of my father, my mother and I were alone on that balcony,
away from my father like in those early days, and I was finally old

enough to let my mother cry. When she could speak again her voice took on a secretive tone: "After my friend Kitty went back to St. John's, there was no one. I had David and you, and I was pregnant with Hal, and your father had joined the army. He didn't have to, you know. He was over thirty, but he did. They all did."

I suddenly saw my mother's repeated stories of the war differently. Now she seemed to me like the ancient mariner, stopping "one in three" hoping always for some kind of closure, some absolution. So I spoke the next words carefully: "You grew up with five sisters and now you had nobody." I knew by the way the tears turned to sobs, and then to grateful nods, and by the sheer joy of being understood that came to her eyes, that I had constructed the right history for my mother.

I went back home to my northern city, after briefly playing therapist to my mother in her sunny retirement place to triumphantly tell my therapist that I had found the truth of why I had such terror in remembering my early childhood: I was being raised by a woman on the edge of a breakdown, a woman pulled from the world that made sense to her, from a mother that came to stay as each baby was born, from a world of sisters having babies of their own, of cousins and school friends, a world where everyone had lived for all their lifetimes so close to their relatives that for a moment, on the way to North Sydney, it must have seemed exciting to be leaving. But that was before the darkness moved in.

I tell the therapist how relieved Kathleen was by her tears, how she then takes pleasure in telling how canny she got at living alone with her babies. She smiles when she says that she yearned for Harold's letters, there alone with us, except there was no home letter delivery and she had to walk quite a way to the mail. She tells of how she would put me in my crib where she knew I was safe, and put David on the floor with his favourite comics and tell him not to move. She would then run all the way to the mailbox (pregnant with Hal by then) and then run all the way back. David was always where she left him and I was always crying in my crib. Sometimes, she tells me, when there was no letter from Harold, she would cry too. Repeating her memory, making it into my story in the therapy session, my cobwebbed dream-child becomes real and I feel my own tears come.

But Kathleen was not the kind of woman to linger long in victimhood. Back in those war days she learned fast how to assert herself, and soon she was successfully warding off the unwanted attentions of males not yet recruited into the forces. When the landlord upped the rent illegally (servicemen's families had their rent frozen by act of Parliament) she and her neighbour persuaded the neighbour's lover, a lawyer, to take the case to court. They won and the landlord was not pleased. Some nights the heat was turned so low that she would take David and me into bed with her and put all the coats she had on top of the three of us to keep us warm. It was wartime and you weren't supposed to complain too much. She says she never cried so much in all her life.

When mother gets to telling stories about North Sydney, her favourite one is about the time Hal was born. As if her life was not difficult enough, she received word, just before the birth, that my father had been given an overseas posting. She didn't even know where it would be, since telling wives such things would inevitably mean the enemy would be sure to know.

Now the one thing Harold and Kathleen had agreed on was that they would never name any of their children after themselves. They were a modern young couple and did not approve of burdening children with their parents' names.

When Hal was born, mother broke the rule. He became Harold James Clarke, Junior, Kathleen being convinced that there would soon be no Senior. With her luck father would be killed in Europe or some godforsaken place in the Pacific. She likes to tell of how she cried when Hal was born, and how she named him for his father and cried some more, and then came home to a little Helen and David, where she found Helen profusely crying, and so she cried some more. When Hal was two months old she went to Truro, Nova Scotia and illegally boarded the troop train from Ontario that was taking my father to Halifax and the war. They had to plead with the conductor who wanted to throw her off. Finally, feeling sorry for the young couple he gave them his private room where they could say goodbye away from the soldiers. They arrived in Halifax and after waving farewell to her husband as he boarded the ship that would take him to war, Kathleen returned to us and the tears the next day. Out in the Atlantic Harold opened his secret orders. Some time passed before the telegram came from him telling Kathleen he had arrived at his overseas posting and it was Newfoundland! He told her to pack her bags and come home.

It wasn't that easy. Months went by while father tried to get the renters out of our home in St. John's. You could not kick out a member of the armed forces in those days and the English officer and his wife who rented our house were having a pretty good war in our home and were not about to move. Dad finally hit on the solution. He told them there was no law saying he couldn't move in with them, which is what he planned to do, wife, kiddies and all. They were out by the end of the month.

Back in North Sydney mother planned her escape. A passenger ferry had been torpedoed between Port aux Basques and North Sydney killing all aboard, so we had to go by airplane, an expensive proposition. The only money they had was in the form of a savings bond, called a victory bond, to be cashed in wartime only in the direst emergency. Kathleen got all dressed up in her best clothing and went to see the bank manager. "Madam," said he (you should hear my mother doing his imperious voice), "Madam, don't you know there is a war on? That savings bond is fighting a war. Do you expect me to take it away from the war effort so that you can have the luxury of living with your husband?" Kathleen went home chastened and tearful.

It was six months after the telegram from Newfoundland when Kathleen finally got her dander up. Why shouldn't she go back to St. John's? There she had a home of her own to raise her children in warmth and comfort, there she had a mother, and yes, all those sisters. Why should her children have to suffer a fatherless childhood? It was 1944 and mother was getting good and sick of the damned war that everyone thought was so much more important than her children. So she got dressed up again. But this time she dressed up the baby, dressed up David and dressed up me. And before she left the apartment she told me, "Helen, when I poke you, you cry." She demonstrated; I obliged. By this time she knew she could depend on me for this one ability at least. And so she went to beg for the reuniting of her family. The bank manager continued to look stern. She poked; I wailed. Baby Hal woke up and cried too, mother cried and even stoic little David, embarrassed as he must have been, joined in the keening. The noise was too much for the bank manager. Kathleen got her victory bond, cashed it and off we flew. I was going home to a place I had never known.

Recently, I was once more visiting my mother, this time in her pleasant apartment west of Toronto where my parents live when not enjoying the winter in Florida. She had just had a knee replacement surgery and I was there for ten days to help her and Dad. We are a good family that way. There's a bit of Newfoundland left in us it seems. My younger sister carries the fullest responsibilities for helping our aging parents, because she lives closest, but my three brothers, their wives, and Richard and I try to do our share. My daughter had taken a day off from her busy Toronto theatre life to come to see us. Mother loves to have a grandchild present when she tells stories of our childhoods. She's at her best then, the grandmother and grandchild laughing and nodding together, the exclamations of "did she really?" and "yes, that's my Mom!" building the story and making us all glow with the present suddenly alive with the past. My role is to sit quietly, exhibiting my chagrin as I am fully revealed as less than parental to my child. Of course, the attention is very flattering. I love it. I feel loved when my mother tells stories about me.

This time her words slipped, telling a story she did not mean to tell. Maybe knee replacements unhinge old memories, ones that don't make such nice stories. Kathleen likes to tell about the strange expressions and mispronounced words and garbled verses that her children mouthed in their early years. My baby brother Peter is famous for not being able to say the sound "le" in words like nipple and table, so that he said "nipploo" and "tabloo." We used to enjoy imitating him. My mother has a bunch of these malapropism stories. Since, as I grew, I graduated from the child who cried too much to the child who talked too much, you can imagine the number she has about me.

I can't believe how I'm procrastinating about getting to the point here. It's that chest feeling again, like I cannot breathe in the present what I do not dare to recall from the past.

Mother likes to draw you into the story by testing your memory: "Helen, do you remember the song you sang on the airplane when we left North Sydney to go home?" "Mares Eat Oats," I answer on cue.

My complicity assured, Mother can now turn her attention to her granddaughter, Erica: "Only your mother said 'mares-e-doats.'" Unexpectedly, she turns back to me: "Do you remember Mary, Helen? Do you remember the girl who looked after you when I was in the hospital having Hal?" I did not remember. This is a new twist in the story. I am alert. Damn it. Where is my pocket tape recorder. (I have been recording my parents off and on for years now.)

Mother continues. "Well anyway, that was during the war you know, Erica, and it was hard to get someone to look after the kids. Any woman who was worth her salt was working in the war factories. And they were joining up too. My youngest sister, your Great-Aunt Olive joined up you know. Did your mother ever tell you that? So there I was in North Sydney and I had no one of my own there you know and I had to hire this fourteen-year-old girl to stay with the children. I was so worried about them that I phoned every day. They used to keep you in the hospital for ten days at that time, and I had no one at home to help me so they kept me longer. So I'd talk to the girl, Mary, and then I'd talk to David and then your mother would get on the phone and all she'd say was, 'She beated me, Mommy, she beated me, she beated me,' over and over again. Your mother used to do that. Put the 'ed' on words like that."

There is silence. Erica looks expectant. Mother, realizing the grammatical point of the story was in danger of becoming lost in some other value, recovers quickly. "I would get Mary back on the phone and I would say, 'Mary, you can't hit Helen,' and she would say, real surly like, 'She won't do what I tell her to.' 'Well you still can't beat her,' I'd say. I'll never forget your mother saying, 'she beated me, Mommy, she beated me.'"

There is silence again, but Kathleen knows now that she must push on, get the story out of this cul-de-sac it seems to have fallen into. She returns to the plot we all know: "Anyway Erica, when I knew we were going home to Newfoundland, and your grandfather would be seeing his kids for the first time in so long, I got them all dressed up. I had bought Helen this lovely little set of matching leggings and coat and bonnet. They were light purple, mauve really. And she looked so cute in them. The cute little mauve bonnet covered her wispy hair so nice. When we got to the airport, the plane was delayed, and they told me to go back home and they would call me later in the day, and I told them that the only home I had was in Newfoundland, and I was not going back to North Sydney, even if they paid me to, not for one minute. So we waited all day in the airport, and the flight didn't leave until the night, and do you know what colour Helen's outfit was at the end of the day?" Like the good actor she is my daughter says the words right along with her Mom Clarke, and with suitable mimicking emphasis: "It was black, black as dirt." They both laugh in their concurrence.

I hardly need to listen to the rest of the story, I've heard it so often: of how I stood in the aisle of the airplane singing "mares-e-doats, and does-e-doats and little lambs-e-divy, a kid'll-e-divy too, wouldn't you?"; I sang it over and over again like some weird, infantile mantra. And how the stewardess called out that we were landing and would someone please make that little girl sit down, but I kept singing, and Kathleen had the baby in her arms and David was being sick in a bag. And how the American army officer in the seat opposite grabbed me and held me tight during the descent. "And your mother screamed at the top of her lungs!"

Erica cannot resist editorial comment: "I bet she did, Mom Clarke, I just bet she did!"

"And she screamed and screamed and that officer held her tighter and despite all his strength he could not make her body bend to sit on his lap. She just stiffened and he couldn't straighten her." It seems there were several landings and take-offs before we got to St. John's, the wartime air service being a bit like the "Newfie Bullet." The American officer was called into service a number of times. Mother says I did not relent, each time giving the man the full benefit of my awesome lungs and hysterical body.

Nothing happens to me for a while after this particular retelling. There is the tightness in the chest of course, but nothing overt. When my ten days of post-operative care of my mother are over I take the tightness back with me to my cottage beside Lake Winnipeg, where I work hard getting reports and papers finished, all the writing that makes up a busy academic life. I work extra hard. My dad once told me that when you are feeling unhappy the best cure is hard work. I work harder. It does not cure. Then one sunny afternoon, as I am sitting on the verandah reading another woman's autobiography, not reading too hard because the fall leaves are beginning to be too beautiful for words, I look up and Richard—who is puttering in the garden—smiles at me because autumn is our favourite season. And then I tell him in plain words about Mary, and I tell him about trying to make my baby brother eat his egg, and I tell him about striking Erica all those years ago. And it begins to be real. I begin to have a history for the pain.

"A history for the pain" should be the nice neat ending for this excavation of my pre-memory childhood. Now that the personal life has been put into words, witnessed by the surrogate therapist (the husband) and made sense of, it is put to rest. Flush it down the toilet like this morning's healthy crap. Gone. Get on with your life. Harping on it will only make people think you are unpleasant, not a nice fiftyish professional lady. Just then I almost wrote, "I'm sorry, but I can't let it go." Sure I could. I could refuse to editorialize, work for the pearl of the short story, whittling, pruning, giving the reader the ambivalent closure that allows you to bring your own ideology to my pain. But I will not. I realize that one of the reasons I am writing this as testimony, as memoir and not as fiction is that I want you to know, dear reader, that this memory work has been hard work, work that changed me, that made me believe and act and think differently. And I want to record that difference. So you may not like this part coming up. You may want to stop reading. Sometimes I skip ahead in a story; you have my permission to do the same. No hard feelings.

It's Mary I won't let go of. In all the stories I read in my pursuit of my understanding of women in this culture I live in, the Marys are the ones who get flushed down that dark hole in the toilet of every story. Their brief appearances are the awkward machinery we use to shut out the history of women. They cower there in every plot, conveniently surly, blameworthy gorgons, unknown and unmourned, sucking up blame like black holes. I must occupy a "Mary" place in other people's stories, maybe in my baby brother's. May the goddess help me, maybe even in my daughter's story.

What I want for Mary is a history. And I can't get it. I can imagine all sorts of psychologically correct causes: abusive father coming up from stinking work in coal mines and beating his kids, or beating his wife while the kids watch. Maybe a mother who had to move Mary from screaming to surly because she was being driven mad with loneliness. Maybe her daughter was the only place she could practice being powerful. Maybe Mary was raped by a priest, or a policeman. Maybe she was just really young, fourteen my mother says, saw everything as a child does, with every cry aimed straight at the heart of little Mary. Maybe hitting me was the only way she knew to keep Kathleen's children from burning down the house, or getting her in trouble with the landlord. Lots of possible causes, no history.

Where is she today? She'd be in her sixties, a decade older than me, maybe still in North Sydney with grown children and grandkids. Do her daughters yearn for their mother's love in the way of daughters that are still children in their hearts? Do they go on and on about their mother, obsessed by the details of her life, unable to explain the bad feelings between them? Do her sons tell their sisters to let it go, don't give so much thinking space to the old woman. I'd like to write a story for Mary, but I can't. I can't say in stories what I really believe, what I know in my bones: In this culture we make girl children grow up too fast and we don't let them grow up at all. I know. I am one.

In the last couple of days while I have been struggling with these few paragraphs about Mary, the television news has been filled with the event of the death of two little boys, murdered it would now appear, by their mother. At first she said a black man took them, the black male being cast as the local version of the boogie man in her part of the world. But now she has confessed to rolling her car into a lake with the little boys still strapped in their child safety seats. People all over are in a terrible state of shock despite the fact that social scientists keep reassuring them that this has been happening since Medea. This case is a bit like the ancient Greek story, since it has a *cherchez l'homme* kind of twist. The mother was a divorcée and the new boyfriend told her that he loved her, but could not bear to live with her what with her ready-made family. I watched the video of her being brought to the courthouse. She's very young-looking to be the mother of two children, and despite everything she's been through in these past days, her hair was tied up in a neat, prettily curled ponytail. It made her look like a fourteen-year-old cheerleader. Of course, cheerleaders have been known to kill.

The shock and the anger of the people interviewed on television made me think about why such a common occurrence—a mother, or any female abusing or killing children—always strikes us as so extraordinary. I'm not arguing against considering the act the profoundest kind of evil, I'm just saying it is hard to understand why we are so shocked by its occurrence. We are never surprised by the violence of men. Every day, it seems, a man murders his kids, his wife, and then maybe himself. It hardly makes the news anymore. Perhaps we expect it from men because they have enshrined so many precedents in their books. From Cronos, through Abraham to the very Lord God of the Christians, males have been trying, often successfully, to do away with or otherwise brutalize their offspring in the most heinous ways imaginable, as a matter of course. The murders are always claimed to be for a good cause, whether it is to confirm a pact with their god or save the souls of people who never asked for any son of any god to be killed for them. These official stories, written down in books, form the basis for legitimatizing the insanity of the crazed guy with the gun in his suburban home, or the fellow with the automatic weapon strolling through the hallways of a school as his victims die around him, and certainly puts the seal of approval on the big men in charge of gathering the next generation of cannon fodder. All these men probably believe in the righteousness of what they are doing, equally vehemently. We certainly know enough about the phenomenon from men's holy books not to be surprised.

But female violence does surprise us. I think it's because women don't have a system going like men, where it's enshrined somewhere: this kind of brutalization and/or killing of the next generation is OK, this other kind is not. We're sort of on our own. We don't have our own holy books. We are outside the law. Like me and Mary in that room with the toilet in North Sydney. Yes. I'm beginning to suspect it was the room with the toilet where we fought our war, where she could not settle whatever score she had to settle, where I withstood her with my screaming voice, or was it my silence, no matter how much she hit. No matter what she did. There. With the toilet. There we were, outlaws, Mary and I. Her. And me. I wonder who has done the most damage since, Mary or Helen? Who suffers as much, remembering or not being able to remember, her or me?

But I'm not here to rank pain. Actually, if the truth be known, I feel quite close to her now, quite in sympathy with little Mary, both of us growing up, or not growing up, female in these terrible times when plots sit out there like Cronos, waiting to eat us alive, or they come swooping down like Zeus, to fuck us over when we least expect it. I'm beginning to talk dirty because this memoir is making me nervous. It is already, only four dozen pages in, on the verge of doing that thing which plots inevitably do: they blame the mother, or the teenaged mother-surrogate in this case. You will notice that I have been careful to break up the blame, tried to disarm it, almost turned it to credit. I have spread it around. There is Kathleen, there is Mary and there is me. And then there is Virginia Woolf, of course, who started it all for me. I don't feel too badly about this vicious circle of blame, because I have forgiven them now, almost everyone in the circle. And I am working at forgiving me. I am writing towards it.

Now I'm beginning to see that bringing in men and their books, may be a dangerous move. The temptation to leap out of any danger of blaming mothers or mother surrogates by blaming that other convenient object of blame, men and their histories, is always there for a feminist like me. But I've been around the circle of plot often enough now to know what happens when I bring men into it, looking for scapegoats. It just gets me recaptured by that other set of plots where everything is so shitty with heroism and fate, and tragic flaws. "Oh," they will sigh, "but we had a war to fight." And then you'll never hear the end of it. They will go on and on, filling up libraries and television channels and whole bloody education systems with their stories. Take the advice of a feminist who has made all the mistakes; don't even open up the subject. Take it from one who has been there; that way lies the real vicious circle. That path is full of Medeas, Jocastas, Lady MacBeths and assorted gorgons and the next thing you know it will be for you that they went to war, and that's just one step from it being your fault. And I realize now that I am calling men "they," as if somehow "they" are the enemy, as if my own husband, brothers, father, the very sons of my womb are not "us." This is the conundrum of feminists who are mothers and the lovers of men: we live with and love our enemies. What I meant to say, before the anger took over, was that "they" have a public record, good and bad, by which to measure their lives. "We" need a history of our own, written by ourselves. You know, stories of the people, by the people, for the people. We need our own measures of accountability, not someone else's plots.

Sometimes the plot circle is so vicious I think maybe the best thing to do is not to write at all. But that would be like telling little Helen not to cry. Or telling Virginia there was no need, not in her privileged place in history, for anger.

When I was rewriting this part of my memoir, tinkering with it, trying for a little grace among all the sharpness, I asked my mother a few more questions about the years in North Sydney to confirm my facts. After she had answered my questions, she sat for a moment, unusually thoughtful for my animated, storytelling mother. "You know," she said slowly, "I have had a very good life, a very happy life, but whenever I think of North Sydney, of those times during the war. . . ." There was a struggle for words, made dramatic because of my mother's usual articulateness, and then she slowly moved her left hand, her index finger hooked, and gently tapped her head, just at her left temple, where I'm told the speech centre is. "Whenever I remember those days, there is a sad place, right here in my head."

There really are moments of truth. My own left hand went up in imitation, as I nodded in what I hoped she would think was sympathy; my finger hooked and set itself down on my left temple, set itself down over the damaged place in my own head.

———————

I don't want to add this bit I'm about to write. I liked this story the way it just ended. And it is a true ending too. My mother's words, her gesture, they really happened. But later, many, many months later something else happened too. While I was with my parents during one of my trips to Toronto, as I was busy preparing lunch for us, the two of them were suddenly standing in the kitchen, side by side against the counter, blocking my way to the table. "Yes?" I said, understanding that this formal pose must mean they had something important to tell me.

"You remember when we told you about your dad joining the Canadian army during the war?"

Oh no, here it comes, they are going to change the story again and ruin my nicely set version of the past. The two of them looking small and old and like they are about to be swallowed by a big cat, make me want to cry. They know I'm writing this memoir and they want to change it. And I don't want to hear. The manuscript has already gone through the distinguished vettors the press has chosen, the editors and the board of directors have given the nod and soon, if the fates will it, the Canada Council will be on side. They can't change it now! I turn away trying not to hear them in my preparation of the vegetables and the sandwiches, steeping the tea just right for their Newfoundland tastes, and cutting up the little sweet for dessert. But, of course, I hear every word.

It goes something like this. Back in the war, my father and mother had been discussing for some time the idea of my dad joining up. But just as his job was running out in North Sydney, there arose a wonderful opportunity. A job opened up in the Newfoundland civil service, a position that he was completely qualified for. You know the kind: it had his name written on it as we say today, and indeed they wired him to come home for an interview, all expenses paid. Dad took the long trip back to St. John's aboard the ferry *Caribou* and the Newfie Bullet. He was sitting reading the paper in the lounge of the Newfoundland Hotel the night before his interview when an old friend came by. The friend was surprised to see him, and even more surprised when he heard his mission. "Everyone on the inside knows that job is already filled by a relative of a commissioner!" As Harold and his friend worked their way through the politics, they realized that my dad's interview may have been honestly arranged, but it was not cancelled when the man with the right relative got the job, because it would look bad, and besides it made a nice cover for the nepotism. The friend begged Dad to go along with the charade since by then they had sat so long talking in the most public part of the hotel that if Harold exposed the sham everyone in the know would guess who had told him the truth and my father's friend, a government man, would be in trouble.

Harold went through with the interview, the long return train ride, the voyage on the darkened *Caribou* through the submarine infested waters, back to Kathleen and the children in North Sydney. He swallowed the insult and went about trying to imagine an alternative future. A week later the *Caribou* was sunk by a torpedo, killing all aboard and Newfoundlanders and Nova Scotians realized the war had come home to them. My father realized that those corrupt bastards in the Newfoundland colonial government had risked his life to cover their dirt. "I was so angry, I said to your mother, 'Kathleen, I'm joining up.'"

While I'm standing there pouring mother's tea, and wondering if I dare point out that joining up to risk your life may not have been the logical response to having your life risked by others, my mother says, "He tried to get out of it when we found out I was pregnant, but the army wouldn't let him."

Is this comedy or tragedy? It would take a Shakespeare to write this story properly, all its male-bonding and betrayal, all its pride and foolishness, all its heroism and self-delusion, all its subtle joinings of public history and individual destiny. It is merely my duty to report what my parents told me. It is not my story. But as I write it in my words, words that I can read over and think about, I see that I may have interpreted my father incorrectly. I assumed he was angry at the big men in Newfoundland. But maybe he was angry at the big men who caused the men and women and children aboard the *Caribou* to die. Maybe he was angry at both. Maybe. I do not know. The only thing I know for sure is the effect on his tiny daughter of his going to war. That's another story. That is my story.

Peace: Daddy's Girl

For the last couple of Monday evenings, as I relax from the writing of the day in the gentle coolness of a Florida winter, I have been watching a television series called "Royal Family" on the American public television network. In my father's genealogical history of our family in North America he makes it quite clear that he thinks the Americans never rebelled against the monarchy, but rather against the oligarchy of merchant/aristocrats that made the colonies' economic life unprofitable. Since these merchants were the same Englishmen that kept Newfoundlanders in poverty, this suits father's historiography very well and reflects the firm bias we still hold against the merchants of south England, and a seemingly contradictory fervent monarchism which has also characterized our family. The loyalty comes partly from our need to separate ourselves as English Protestants from the Irish Catholics, a later immigration wave to Newfoundland, but it is also founded on our need to hold on to some part of that English tradition. We may have resented and despised the English, but the royals were always exempt. It is ironic to me, that as the royal family less and less represents the values of my childhood, they become more and more fascinating to some folks on this side of the Atlantic.

My childhood memories are of the wartime princess who later would become the queen of peace. Now, as I watch the old news clips with the cynicism of age, her teenage self who once smiled bravely into my four-year-old soul is cast into a kind of late-twentieth-century "impostorhood" much like my own. But back then, in the forties it was different.

53

When I was a very young girl, maybe six or seven, my Uncle Sam came home from Boston. I know it sounds too good to be true that I had an American Uncle Sam, but I did. Lots of little Newfoundland girls had uncles in Boston, and a goodly number were named Samuel; the particular kind of Newfoundlanders I come from, the Methodist kind, liking to name sons after biblical worthies. The "pipeline" to Boston, as my father likes to call it, or the "Boston States," as it used to be called in Newfoundland—as if the whole of that vast country was contained in one city—as indeed it often was for Newfoundlanders—had been in place for over three hundred years, and through it, in hard times, went some of the best and most talented of Newfoundland's young people. My own maternal grandmother, Olivia, went to Boston, met her Newfoundland husband and begged him to make their future in the States. But he wanted to be a sea captain and command a sailing vessel and felt he couldn't rise to such heights in the stratified Bostonian world. In Carbonear the Osmonds were known as "proud" (which meant they liked there to be no doubt about their respectable rank) and my maternal grandfather's choice of a house, a small piece of land to inherit back home, and a known position in the community—not to mention the possibility of his own boat—was a surer guarantee that nobody would disrespect him than could be counted on in entrepreneurial America, despite its much greater financial opportunities. Like the proverbial "barrels from Boston," filled with the charity of used clothing from richer American relatives, the young couple came back through the pipeline to settle at home and make the future that contained my mother.

There was one American idea that had no chance no matter how often it came down the pipe from Boston, and that was the idea that the royal family was a tool of our oppression. I remember my Uncle Sam standing with my father beside the piano in our home on Craigmillar Avenue, and asking when Newfoundland was going to see the light and join the States. My Dad raised his glass of rum and pointed it at the calendar hanging on the wall where a picture of the young Princess Elizabeth smiled at us: "I tell you what Sam; join me in a toast. Here's to the girl who will be the first lady of the Commonwealth one day." Uncle Sam laughed and I ran to the kitchen to tell my mother of my father's remarkable élan.

My remarkable father and Princess Elizabeth were basically what made me the girl I was then. And they both linger in me today. Despite the disillusionment of bringing adult eyes to my idols, despite the unfashionableness of such types as my father and the queen in our end-of-millennium world, they are, I am afraid, part of me.

"Lillibet" she was called by her little sister "Margaret Rose," and during the war when she spoke to the "children of the empire" on the radio she told us about duty and being good, and helping our parents during these difficult times. Lillibet grew up during the later years of the war, unlike me, who remained an unempowered kid. She learned how to drive and tend a very large military truck; all I got to do was watch a young corporal in a jeep swing up to our door, shove his gear stick back and forth impressively, revving his (no doubt symbolic as well as real) engine, while waiting for my father the army captain to emerge. Off they would roar in that beautiful jeep to the mysterious duties of defending our lives from the enemy. Newfoundland was close to the war zone of Atlantic shipping, we had blackout blinds at our windows and there was a submarine net across the mouth of St. John's harbour; all this lent authority to the jeep, the driver and my father who ran the radar network that protected our shorelines.

I stood in their dust while Princess Elizabeth got to drive around everywhere in her truck. She would drive up to Buckingham Palace where Princess Margaret Rose was having a go at a piano concerto (she was the pretty and artistic one) and off they would romp with their mom and dad, the king and queen, to have a picnic. I had seen them all together at the picnic on the newsreels. Despite the fact that Margaret Rose was prettier and could play the piano, it was Elizabeth who, when the wind whipped the king's hair in his eyes, reached up and pushed the lock of hair from her father's brow. Seeing the gesture now on the old film, enhanced, slow motioned, repeated by the makers of the television documentary for its full effect, it still tugs memories, pulls them whole and powerful, up through my gut and out onto the page, memories of a time when little girls learned to worship their fathers who were standing fast, against the enemy.

Actively and passively in all the ways we lived our days back then in the forties and fifties, we middle-class, white girls were made into daddys' girls. According to Freud this identification with the father is supposed to be an inevitable growing-up process, but as everyone knows nowadays, Freud was not describing archetypal truths, merely upper- and middle-class turn-of-the-century Viennese. But in some ways he could have been describing the ambitious, upwardly mobile, middle-class world which my parents were becoming a part of in those post-World War II times, the times that I now begin to believe define the spirit of the century.

You see, I don't think it will be all the dreadful violence of our wars, with their spectacular evils, that will really be important to those looking back from the distance of the next century. Wars will look like false starts towards a change that we now call by many names, but which really took on speed in those fat years following the two big wars, when, once we thought of something better to do with the new technologies than to kill one another, we all settled down to becoming prosperous. We became economical about the use of war, finding it handy as the short fix for disciplining the so-called "developing" countries, or even more economically, we showed the underdog nations how to do it to each other. When the next millennium writes of us it may, if it has any sense, assess our disgusting "world" wars only in terms of their human and ecological waste, their economic inefficiency, and their sheer waste of time. I think it will be the complexities that the new technologies have brought to the ways we think about class, gender and race, about wealth, poverty and culture that will be seen as the important different direction of our time.

What has all this got to do with Princess Elizabeth, my dad and me? I've read a number of autobiographies by little girls like me, ones whose daddies went loyally to war and later went to the business of making their way in the world of peace with equal single-minded devotion. These daddies are all of a shape: they were absolutely devoted to work, work in the name of being a good provider, in the name of making up for lost time after the pinching of the Depression and the debacle of the war. This meant that they were hardly ever home. That was the big difference between them and the middle-class English Victorian families, those that we read about in the great book tradition where we get our idea of middle-class from. Middle-class Victorian fathers were always around, underfoot, managing the affairs of the house like regimental generals. Poor Elizabeth Barrett could hardly take a pee without her father knowing it. But by the 1940s the middle class wasn't what it used to be because they had lost the servant class to tend them. In fact, some of the servant class was becoming the middle class. Those Victorian dads had servile multitudes working for pennies a day at the office or store, and platoons of maids keeping the household in order. They probably dropped in at their offices between ten and two to survey their professional or commercial kingdoms and had loads of time at home to lay down the law on everything from what the kids ate at breakfast to what went into their little heads.

My middle-class daddy is of another kind. Germaine Greer called her book about her father, *Daddy, we hardly knew you* and indeed we did not. This made worship easier. Mothers also helped. During the war they kept promising us everything would be better when daddy came home. We yearned and yearned and yearned in a great collective yearning that has taken decades to undo. Some of us, too young to adopt positively to the ideology of war, hinted at something like fault as I unconsciously did, repeating over and over again my wail of misery at the window while my dad vanished down the path of war: "My daddy gone, neber took me." I hope you noticed that the second clause of that sentence is an accusation as well as an editorial comment, a prescient judgment on patriarchy's abandonment of its girl children that I now feel nourished my embryonic feminist selfhood: "My daddy gone, neber took *me*." But most people over the age of two accepted the idea that the war was a holy one and that our very families depended on all the daddies going. Then when Daddy came home, it wasn't so much work as usual as it was work more than usual. After the war, mothers explained that, too. Mine pronounced regularly that we were very lucky to have Harold Clarke for a father, as he was educated, employed, and brought home all his money for the benefit of his family, while others, she hinted darkly, did not. I suppose she was so grateful to have a regular life after her own scary wartime years that she rather blew him out of proportion compared to the men around him. For years I thought my father a little too good for St. John's, Newfoundland. I found his true image on the silver screen and it took me well into my adulthood to admit that my childhood father did not look, act and speak exactly as Henry Fonda did in the heroic Hollywood movies that I went to every Saturday as a child.

Of course these heroes of peacetime were being driven by devils of their own. I know my father was. It had to do with the tenuous hold on middle-class status of that first generation of white, male technocrats to which my father belongs. A generation or two before he might have gone to the fishery like all his ancestors or if by some stroke of luck he had completed grade school he would have been one of those minions in the Victorian patriarch's business, working out his life in the bad pay of some St. John's merchant baron (the St. John's merchants having replaced the Englishmen at the task of oppressing Newfoundland fisherman). What made the difference for my dad was higher education and a keen desire for the knowledge of the new sciences and technologies.

In a small way the new middle class began with my paternal grandfather, who, through sheer talent, hard work and brains along with the convenient opportunity of the growth of railways, broke from the subsistence life of fishing that should have been his lot and apprenticed as a stone mason, eventually becoming a foreman in charge of building bridges and trestles all over Newfoundland. He did all this with no education. He told my dad that he went to school for only two days in his entire life. After being sent home for some prank, he never returned. His wife taught him the rudiments of reading and writing after their marriage. But with his success the family had obviously got a taste of what a little knowledge could get you in the new century, because the story of my father's climb to higher education is legendary among the relatives.

There is some disagreement as to who should actually get credit for my father's success. Some relatives give credit to his older brother Leonard for giving him board and room when he did his first college years in St. John's and with instilling in him the fear of God in ways only older brothers can do to younger brothers. Others have assured me that being a younger child he had opportunities the others did not. Some even hint darkly that others may have been deprived for his sake. I find some evidence in my father's writings that he may have been the favourite of his father's later years and thus may have felt a duty, after his father's early death, to prove himself a worthy son.

My mother, on the other hand, insists on the self-made man version of Harold and has assured me over and over that he sent himself to college, paying board to his older brother, having won the highest money prize available to a Newfoundlander, the Jubilee Scholarship, which would eventually take him to the "mainland" for his last two years of education. My father's science degree from Dalhousie University became quite famous for a while among the older generation in Victoria, Newfoundland. When my sister went to see the ancestral village some years back, she met an old timer and tried to explain which of the dozens of male Clarkes that had gone away was her father. She finally listed enough ancestors for the old fellow to exclaim, "Not the Clarke boy that got all the heducation!" This comment was made decades ago; now it would seem half the village is going to university and nobody says "heducation."

My father's "heducation" didn't do him much good at first. Late in his final year he was struck by tuberculosis—probably because his resistance to disease was lowered as a result of selling his blood to supplement his scholarship. He was sent first to a hospital and then later home to Newfoundland to recover. In some ways tuberculosis had the kind of social stigma then that AIDS has now. It certainly narrowed my father's prospects. He never applied for a Rhodes Scholarship as he had planned and although he went back the next year and challenged the exams and finished at the top of the class he did not get job offers. In those days the top few science graduates at Dalhousie were offered jobs with the blossoming American petroleum companies. Father was not. They said it was because he hadn't graduated in his proper year, but then it might have been because the health record would make immigration to the U.S. or Canada virtually impossible. Later the Canadians were quick enough to give him landed immigrant status when they needed educated young men for the war effort. But as it was, he went home in the middle of the Depression, with all that education, and helped his mother on the garden farm that supplied much of the family's needs. He applied for every school teaching position up and down the east coast of Newfoundland and prayed that something else would come along to save him from a life in the profession I now call my own. And it did. He began his career in communications, first in cable, post and telegraphs, and during the war in radar, and later, when the century began to take on the shape of a communications revolution, his knowledge base expanded to the intricacies of what came to be called telecommunications.

But in those first years the early setbacks must have left him always with a very realistic sense of how little security bright technocrats whose grandfathers were fishermen actually have. The war must have grafted that extra bit of survivor mentality onto an already driven desire, while an overheated, but underrealized career ambition did the rest. Then, when Newfoundland's confederation with Canada brought him a broader field of ambition, his career took off like the very rockets that would later carry the giant communications satellites his new country has become so fond of shooting into space in the name of national unity.

When I was doing therapy in my late thirties and early forties, trying to find out why I was going crazy for no apparent reason, I rarely spoke of my father. I was pretty hung up on my mother at that time.

But once, after years of therapeutic sessions, when I had already begun to write (had actually published one short story and was daring to think that I was writing a novel), my therapist asked me why I was so uncertain about my writing. I had just finished confessing how hard it had been, still was (still is) to be with writers, to think of myself as a writer, to get rid of the feeling that I still always have with other writers, that I am an impostor. Suddenly—and most uncharacteristically for me, who always found a significant story of my mother at any prodding at all—I started to tell the therapist about the time my father blew the top off of Pyramid Mountain. I must admit that I elaborated a bit, because I could see that—unlike the carefully sympathetic, but neutral stance cultivated during my stories of my mother—my therapist was being drawn into the romance of my father. Who wouldn't be? It's a good story and I think I told it well.

I will try to tell it more plainly here. It seems my father was supervising the building of the first telecommunications microwave system across Canada, and his engineers were having some trouble with the portion through the Rockies, west of Edmonton, Alberta. The only way to avoid a very circuitous route was to put a transmitter on top of Pyramid Mountain, but Pyramid Mountain was true to its name and there was no place to put a transmitter. My father convinced the powers-that-be to let him blow thirty feet off the mountain rather than spend the extra sixty or more millions it would cost to go around it. The government of the day being in favour of quick solutions and, father having been careful to keep the whole plan quiet so that the ecological types that were then just beginning to bother business did not hear about it, agreement was quickly reached. The conservationists did find out at the last minute, but it was too late. It was years later in Winnipeg—his grandchildren playing around his feet in the ornate decor of the fur-trader nostalgia of the Fort Garry Hotel's Factor's Dining Room—that Harold told me the story of how he had outwitted the green gurus.

To be fair, my father is all for managed forestry and thinks that what has happened to the Newfoundland fishery should be a lesson to us all in how not to manage a resource. However, he does consider knocking off the tops of mountains a reasonable act of resource management. It's simple and has no readily apparent side effects, such as polluted streams or destroyed animal habitat, to pinch the conscience. No floods or weather changes will come back to plague us. Best of all, the bottom line, as businessmen like to say, was that it would be cost-effective. An argument for aesthetics, that a thing of natural beauty is a joy forever, would not cut much granite with Harold. And besides, he really liked doing it. He liked saving the sixty million, he liked convincing the Ottawa mandarins, he liked fooling the conservationists, and he liked the idea of the big blast. I think he also likes the fact that the top of Pyramid Mountain will always be slightly blunted, as if someone had taken a few blocks off one of Egypt's famous monuments. My father is a man of his age; he liked to build things, and like men of his age who were builders, he also found he had to tear down.

When I told this anecdote in my therepy session there was a long pause—almost as if the therapist would have preferred to be mentoring my father—before professionality finally forced the question: "And what does all this have to do with your writing, Helen?" I knew the answer, although I had never thought about it before. I knew the answer then and I know it now. I answered truthfully: "I'm afraid that no matter how good I get at writing I'll never be able to equal blowing the top off Pyramid Mountain." Did my therapist begin to furiously take notes to hide the smile that must have been as irresistible as yours may well be right now, dear reader, as Dr. Freud's would be if he were still with us. This story can certainly be read as a rather amusing form of penis envy.

I want to be honest. Everyone knows nowadays that Freud's concept of penis envy is just another way of saying that people with penises do have advantages in a culture they made for themselves. They have envious privileges and, yes, I do envy my father. I even envy my brothers. I sometimes envy men I would not want to be for a million dollars. It is not so much their privilege as males, their opportunities in the world or even their higher standard of living that I envy. I have learned to place more value on the skills I have gained from having to tactically disguise my goals and fight with a guerilla cunning just to steal some of that male privilege to make my way in the world. I value learning to be a resistance fighter—crossing the lines to mingle with the enemy— disguised as a chubby, older lady with bizarre taste in clothes. So I have no need for that kind of simple envy of privilege and the possibilities for success it makes possible. And do not for a moment entertain the thought that I envy the easy ruthlessness that inevitably accompanies male privilege, for I have had my own moments of ruthlessness and have some tearing-down intentions of my own. Sometime ago I accepted my portion of Virginia Woolf's symbolic guineas and I intend to use them as cannily as I can for exactly the purposes she proposed. I am not faint-hearted with ordinary envy. No, what I envy in my father and other men is their comfort with who they are. I am convinced they do not feel like impostors. I am also convinced that nothing I will ever write, even though I may blow the tops off people's heads as Mr. Kafka said good writing should, will give me the pleasure of fulfillment of my sense of self that my father received for his work in the world. With each accomplishment I continue to feel like an impostor.

It's that sense of being a fish out of water, always a false self, never quite at home in any of my multitude of roles, that I sometimes resent. These feelings are very old, must have begun sometime way back, during the psychic emergency that was the war for little daddies' girls, or in the days of the peace that began when my daddy, looking as kingly as Lillibet's daddy, took me from my bed the night of the celebration of victory in Europe, and held my little four-year-old body high so I could see the fireworks over the harbour of St. John's. The evening climaxed with sky rockets that etched the silhouettes of the king, the queen and the princesses high above our collective gasps of happiness. I did not feel like an impostor then. I felt at home on the front verandah of my father's house on Craigmillar Avenue, in St. John's, Newfoundland, oldest colony of the British Empire, held in his protective arms, the terrible wartime over forever. I have not felt so much at home since.

This anecdote about V-E Day which I have just related to you is a lie. Sometimes my word processor runs away with me. My Microsoft goes soft on some microevents, so to speak. Weak joke. I'm writing weak jokes because I'm embarrassed at my lie. I was not swept into my father's arms on V-E Day. I was sent to bed before the fireworks started because I was only four years old and they were to occur after my bedtime. But the adults were out on the verandah below my window so I woke. My brother David was with them. Repeat: My older brother, only three years my senior, was out on that verandah being privileged by adult company. Although the view of the fireworks was pretty good from my upstairs window I howled and complained until they couldn't hear themselves think and they let me come down to join them. The actual explosion of the flare that etched the faces of the royal family was accompanied by my surly, self-isolation at the corner of the verandah. It was the beginning of a history in which I always find myself let in to whatever company I have joined by the power of sheer volubility—oh, let her in to shut her up. Once inside, I remain unwelcome in my heart.

By telling you the truth of that night of fireworks, rather than a neatly constructed lie of my father's arms, I hope to avoid the tempting plot trap of searching for a "lost paradise" in childhood. Let's admit it, for us little daddies' girls of the wartime there never was a paradise to lose. And what's more, free of happy beginnings, maybe I can free myself of expectations of happy endings. I need that because I have days when I feel as the old woman who is Lillibet must feel in this time of exhaustion at the end of our century, when as queen her most important task seems to be doing damage control in her naughty children's lives. Not that my children need much of this, but in my job I seem to be involved in more and more intellectual damage control, trying to undo some of the vile effects of growing up in an ideology of individualism contrarily developed in a time of enormous social security. Some of the young people I teach never had a toothache that wasn't immediately fixed. Correction: they have never needed to experience a toothache since their parents had dental plans that emphasized preventive measures. Now they want us all to fly without a safety net. Their desires for a big piece of capitalist pie are sugar-coated by an unreasonable expectation that the communal security systems will stay right in place while they act in ways that will inevitably destroy the systems. The young are a confusing mix of greed and idealism, and straightening them out intellectually is painful, discouraging work and the literary texts I am expected to use are not always what I require to do the job. I often feel like an impostor doing this work—nobody ever told me this was part of my job description. The queen must wonder sometimes how she got into this late twentieth-century mess. Nobody told us daddies' girls that we would have to do all this gritty, dirty, public mothering. And the need for it keeps growing. The starving desire for unnoticed, self-effacing, thankless maternality seems to know no class limitations, no income-level cutoff, no racial boundaries.

But it is not just the effort of undoing the belief in the dominant ideology while working inside one of its chief bastions that makes me feel like an impostor. I think part of the feeling of impostorhood, at least for me, comes from the dichotomy I must have experienced between the world we—as a newly middle-class, upwardly mobile, progressive family—believed in and the world I actually lived in. You see, Newfoundland, although almost as class-conscious as the very Brits that fueled Mr. Karl Marx's analysis, is a place which, through its volatile economic history of feast and famine, of "shirtsleeves to shirtsleeves in three generations," and its long memory for dubious family connections, constantly makes mock of the permanency of class.

And then there are the women. It seems to me that neat theories of class based on the accomplishments and privileges of men, depend on women who take their appropriate places in their fathers' and husbands' worlds as hapless victims or princesses of privilege. This was not exactly the case in the Newfoundland of my memory. I have come to believe that if Marx had met my grandmother Clarke he would never again have been quite so clear in his thinking about class analysis. In fact, if he had spent one afternoon cup of tea, one evening glass of blueberry wine with Nanny Clarke, as we called her, he would definitely have not said that dreadful line about religion being the opiate of the people. For my grandmother, religion, in particularly the unestablished forms, such as her own Methodism and her father's late-in-life devotion to the Salvation Army, were forms of personal empowerment that helped free the proletariat from their oppressor's hold.

My father writes in his instructive family history that Newfoundland society long lacked order and good government. Apparently a great uncle of mine on my mother's side was smothered to death in a snow bank by rowdy boys and no justice was ever attempted. Nobody came from St. John's to investigate, no arrests were made. Maybe the family didn't try. To bring yourself to the attention of the merchant-controlled powers, in the mind of the much-suffering Newfoundlander, might not be the better part of valour. A three-hundred-year history of dispossession, oppression and the almost entire absence of the famed British justice system which was supposed to have been the mother country's great gift of empire, meant that Newfoundlanders, outside of St. John's at least, had no institutions except what they made themselves, rough-shape them as they might. So, like the blacks in the southern United States, they made religion serve for nearly every public social institution. But there was a difference: my grandparents, when they raised their voices in the safety of their churches, did not sing their hymns with the heart-wounding beauty of those former slaves; instead of song they made speech; they gave personal testimony to the power of God in their lives, testimony that rivalled the rhetoric of any English parliament.

My great-grandfather, Nanny Clarke's father, had spent his early life in drunkenness and debauchery, a common solution to career reverses in Newfoundland as in other places, like Ireland, where the Empire had been able to extend its oppressive neglect for too many centuries. In his latter years my great-grandfather took the pledge. He had done so countless times before and failed, for as we would say in our jargon of today, he had no vehicle for self-empowerment, no ideology with which to buttress his individual resolve. But when he joined the Salvation Army, a belief system mobilized itself in his drink-fogged brain and he went from being a man who had torn the very boards from his wife's house to buy drink, to being a man who the community could count on for charity, a humble heart, and personal testimony that could spellbind the frequenters of the Salvation Army meeting house. He lived with my grandmother and her husband as he aged and was an enormous domestic help to the daughter whose life he had once made miserable.

The lesson of the power of religion for good in individual lives was not lost on my grandmother. Choosing the method of Methodism over the enthusiasm of the Army, she adhered to the stern but successful credos of hard work, storing up against the famine of tomorrow, duty to your roles as parent, spouse, and member of the larger community. It made her strong, made her strong enough to educate her illiterate husband, made her strong enough to raise children who were not beaten by the wicked world that would have kept them poor. In fact, I'm beginning to think that Marx was being foolishly bourgeois to make that snotty remark about religion being the opiate of the people. You can only say such trite things when, like Marx and me, you have the benefit of a secular form of education and can rely on middleclass institutions of culture to give you the tools of selfhood.

Now despite the fact that I am a good daughter of the irreligious, late-capitalist middle-class, who absorbed the worship of the personal father as the twentieth-century replacement for God the Father, my actual childhood kept throwing the Nanny Clarkes of this world in my face to confound my ideology. How could the sun rise and set in quite so unqualified a fashion over the self-made-man-ness of my father when in our lives was a woman to whom he himself deferred with the fearful contriteness of a priest in the temple of the goddess? And please don't get the idea that I sat daintily on my affectionate grandmother's lap absorbing love like mother's milk. My grandmother would have had a measure of healthy contempt for the lapped idiocies of the devoted and mindless grannies foisted on us by the mass media of our times.

My grandmother ran a farm. I remember as a very small child, no more than five, being taken into her back kitchen, the summer kitchen, where she explained to me—in a tone of voice that seemed to assume a frightening maturity on my part—how the various foods there were gathered and processed, what their future purposes were and how long they would likely last. Everything in that room was her product; many of the raw materials came from her farm. She had been a widow since her husband's early death, and she had learned how to make sons and daughters work as hard as she did.

My father recalls that as a young teenager he occasionally used to take a forbidden break from weeding the vegetable garden to have a leisurely swim in the stream that bordered their property. My grandmother would always find him, pull him bodily from the water, give him a few hits with a switch to drive home the lesson of God-fearing hard work, and send him back to the vegetables. Work, for yourself and your God, was how you earned status in my grandmother's world. Work included the careful cultivation of the intelligence that God had given you.

By the time I was five, when my father had achieved the success of a steady job, a home of his own and a healthy family, he was allowed, on our visits to her home in Victoria village, to spend some time in the afternoons reading in his mother's parlour, a place mostly used for the visits of clergy and the laying out of the dead. Despite the special place work had in her belief system, despite the fact that she was surrounded by and adherent to a rather puritanical form of Methodism, her house was a beautiful place, filled with the ornate furniture of another age, furniture bought by her maternal grandfather, Daniel Lacy, who was rumoured to have been a pirate, or at least a privateer. It must have bothered her to have such rich articles, but had them she did. She and her husband had lost all their savings in the bank crash of 1895 and to build their house they had taken apart the old Lacy house in Crocker's Cove and rebuilt it on their land in Victoria. The furniture came with it of course, and stood in every room, impressing the likes of me with my grandmother's wealth, but probably reminding her of a more nasty legacy. Here in this transplanted house, my father tells me, she welcomed the society of the day—the villagers and the greater world—with her excellent blueberry wine, an ambrosia my father remembers as tasting like a fine claret.

But I knew nothing of my grandmother's social skills, nor her blueberry wine. Being a child, who was never allowed to go much past the kitchen, I remember only glimpses of the imposing curved legs of the dining room table, the silky red glow of the chaise lounge in the parlour. In my later memories, my paternal grandmother rather overwhelmed me so that I thought of her as too strict, too hard. This stems from the fact that when she was older and unable to live alone she lived with us, and my memories of her out of her own home are less pleasant. The sound of her reading her Bible aloud was so foreign to us that the family used to defuse the power of her voice by joking behind her back that Nanny Clarke was studying for her finals. She was. Indeed, she told us herself that she was preparing to meet her maker.

When I was about seven my mother had her first knee surgery and could not bend to wash the kitchen floor. It had not yet occurred to my mother, as it certainly would later in life, that male upper-body muscle is delightfully suited to the tasks of floor scrubbing, so I, being female and able-bodied, was identified as the only possible helper. Kathleen sat in the corner of the kitchen encouraging me, directing me to attack the floor in sections, washing with soap, rinsing the rag in fresh water, wringing it out and wiping dry. With each laborious square I completed, she praised my sloppy efforts as wonderful, hoping that my flagging energies would get me all the way round the kitchen. Unfortunately, Nanny Clarke, who never did think that Kathleen was very good at teaching proper domestic science, arrived on the scene and began to critique the work, pointing out that "the child" was not wringing the cloth out properly, was leaving streaks of soap and the floor would be wet for the rest of the day. My mother argued leniacy on the basis of my youth, but Nanny Clarke set about to give me proper instruction. The woman who had raised four sons and three daughters to be efficient workers was not about to let her seven-year-old grandaughter lapse into the habits of a "lick and a promise" that were good enough for Kathleen. I, in one of the spiteful gestures that were to become typical of me in my teenage years, threw down the sopping washrag and made a grand exit telling the old woman to do it herself. She no longer could, nor could my mother, age and injury preventing them. Since my mother was angry at Nanny for having driven away her only worker she refused to call me back and I got away with my little gesture of defiance.

It was hard for my grandmother to live with her daughter-in-law; my mother, who had been raised by a gentler mother, was often intimidated and frustrated by Nanny Clarke. I remember Kathleen telling me that she used to have to hide my father's rum bottle—from which he could afford only highly infrequent sips—so that my temperance-society grandmother would not be enraged that her son had turned to drink. (Blueberry wine, it seems, did not count as drink.)

When I came to write of my paternal grandmother in my earlier writing life, I wrote in the expected way that my definitions as a daddy's girl required. She was a bit of an old witch in my description I'm afraid, as all powerful women must be in the patriarchally defined minds of girls. My father, in one of his rare comments on my writing, corrected me—rather gently I thought at the time—by telling me about the grandmother I couldn't remember. He told me about her charities, her position in the community, her pride in work well done, and especially about her intelligence and articulateness, even her humour in conversation.

"Of course she could be a little self-righteous, as when she lectured the poor on her work ethic while giving them produce from her garden. But she did work harder than everyone else. What you couldn't know about her as a young girl was her intelligence. People loved to come to her house just to talk with her, and you know, despite her firm religion, when she spoke of the world, she had a really healthy cynicism. Your grandmother, you know, was a bit of an intellectual in her way, and like all intellectuals she was also a bit of a skeptic about man and his world."

That was it. I was a convert. I suddenly revised my whole view of my grandmother, accepted her as my most significant ancestor and have begun to cultivate her as my proto-feminist precursor. This must make the poor old lady turn in her grave. Or maybe not.

It is a pleasant irony for me to think that I can revise my paternal grandmother to give me the ancestress that all feminists need these days to act as counters to the insidious pull into the laws of the father that many of us suffer from as daddies' girls, by which we strive to be even better at our jobs than our daddies were, and hope that by doing so we will inherit his power, his language. Being a feminist who has decided to stay inside the system is a tricky act, full of ironies and betrayals. Here I have made my father's defence of his mother the source of my revision of his story. He defends his mother, I revise his words to make her my own. A bit like stealing fire.

I have never asked my father enough questions about his mother; I will have to be careful when I do. Too much obvious curiosity, too many inquiries might put him on the alert to my subversion of his version of his mother. I will have to play my cards carefully, watch for the small slips where the right sympathetic chuckle or sigh of regret might make him speak what he does not intend to say. I will have to be patient too, letting the talk of one day ruminate to get at the revelation of the next. Easy enough to be Sheherazade spinning stories to save your life; I will have to get my father to tell stories to make my life. This is going to be risky. This is going to be fun. This is the life for which impostorhood has trained me.

Since I wrote those last words I have flown around the continent, doing the business that academics on sabbatical do—going to conferences, checking in on graduate students—and managed three days to visit my parents, drove them over the tangle of freeways to Toronto, so we can have dinner with my son and his wife and see my daughter in a play. My subversive agenda was, as I have said, Nanny Clarke. But I was not to get my father's mother, even with my bag of feminist tricks, as easily as I imagined. My father will talk to me hour upon end about the past; he is always willing and has an excellent memory for detail. But as he ages his concerns narrow. On this occasion my every leading question about the grandmother whose midlife I wanted to rescue from the 1920s and 1930s took my father to his own life, to its traumatic hours, to its settlements with history. I try to get to the woman who was Ann Clarke through her son's memory of the Depression years, but what I get instead is a reminiscence of the days at Dalhousie, when illness drove him home. I try again, asking what her situation was during the war—who was at home? My aunt Bertha died of tuberculosis—how was that for Nanny Clarke? Was she more alone as the population of Victoria declined with the dispersal of its sons and daughters to wartime service and jobs? Instead, I hear the story of the disillusionment of a young college graduate, fed on empire and liberal humanism, as he remembers the betrayals, the crimes, the sheer greed that his job as secret censor of the cross-Atlantic cables allowed him to observe. "The things that happened to people just as a result of one cable sent, was horrible. It was awful to read it all, every day, to see the way the world worked for people with money." And we are off on another tack entirely, my father lecturing me on a public history I know all too well, the private story of my grandmother lost to me again.

I will plan other occasions to capture his memory to my purpose, but I will not hold out too much hope. We have been urging father for some time now to quit writing of public history and family genealogy and write his memoirs, write his life of risk and achievement tossed on the oceans of technological advance. It seems he has accepted his children's advice and is writing his memoirs as he speaks to me, finally telling me his life at the moment I have learned to want his mother's life. I do not think I will get much more of her though, not from him.

Like the rest of the brave band of women memoirists I am reading in this moment of apocalypse, I shall have to invent my foremothers for myself. I will try to find scraps of truth; a memory or two has spilled off the ends of Kathleen's and Harold's stories over the years. And for concrete details there is the genealogy so carefully prepared by my father.

At the back of my father's family-history book there is one of those doubled genealogy pages, one which spreads out from the central point of us five siblings, David, Helen, Harold, Katherine and Peter. On this portrait of our family we are enclosed top and bottom by mother and father respectively. Kathleen and Harold get their own large spaces, shield-like, star-billing so to speak. Then, placed on two ribbon-like strands on the sides of the two parental shields are the names of each of my parents' parents, mother's father and mother, father's father and mother. Their spaces are just large enough for their dates of birth, marriage and death. I have the chart beside me as I write and realize suddenly, at this moment, with a laugh, what I—despite my feminist alertness—have missed until now: the gendering of the tree. My father's mother is not part of his sign, instead she sits beneath my mother's sign. Suddenly I understand what I am seeing. The chart is divided into male lines and female lines. Even though at each generation male and female names appear, they are segregated. The ancestors spread out to left and right, mother's side, father's side, like wings that hold us airborne. At the top of the page in a large space is my mother's sign. Below her are her five children, springing from the belly of her sign, so to speak. Attached to her sign, almost as if they were the ribbony limbs of her body opening wide to birth us, are the two grandmothers, her mother, and my father's mother. The two grandfathers spring up from my father's sign at the bottom of the page, almost as if they were balloons of thought. So there under "husband's mother" is Ann Lacy Butt, occupying half of a little heraldic flag, the other half belonging to my maternal grandmother. Women who had little time, perhaps little desire to enjoy each other's company in life, might smile to see themselves neatly penned by my father onto this maternal ribbon. Ann's essential dates are given, born 20-1-1875, married (and gained the name Clarke) 25-4-1896 and died 18-9-1953. I remember that September day of her death well, since I was considered too young to face the rigours of her funeral. My brother David, a mature fifteen, after a long parental parley, went along. I cried at the kitchen window, once more untaken, and knew in the honesty of my twelve years that I was crying not for my grandmother, but for my own increasing exclusion from my father's life. My youngest brother, Hal, recently told me that he went to the funeral also. If he is right, then I have suppressed the gendered cause of my tears. If it had been a funeral of Ann's time even my mother would have been left at home, the puritan family being afraid that women might cry at funerals.

Ann's time. There are some hints in my father's "Notes on the South Side Butt Family" as to what kind of times she lived in. Desperate times for a young girl, whose father—the South Side Butt who married "up" to the Crocker's Cove Lacy family—was an alcoholic. Ann's mother was a fragile thing, never a match for her drunken husband and her two drunken sons. To see Ann's life more fully in the context of her times, I need to go back further along that branching genealogy tree to her grandparents. Grandparents must have been important to a girl who grew up watching her mother being beaten by her six-foot-five husband, a man enraged at jibes about his height in the pub, coming home to take it out on his wife. Ann and her sister Lizzie witnessed daily the poison of a man too big for his place in life. Her brothers were no help; much older than her, growing every terrifying day more like their father, they eventually tore the very hemlock boards from off the Lacy house and sold them for drink. Certainly she would find no help in her mother who, being raised in a well-to-do family, pampered by safety, had none of the survival strategies a woman needs to counter a husband bent on taking out his disappointment with life on her. Her own mother cowed, her maternal grandmother early in her grave, Ann would find no suitable models for behaviour in her grandfathers. Her grandfather Lacy was supposed to have had a shady past, a pirate or a slaver by some reckonings, but my father locates his probable source of wealth as that of a privateer, commissioned by the British to do to their enemies what a pirate does without commission. Still, not a likely attraction for a young, abused girl. On her father's side there was her grandfather Butt who seems unexceptional at anything, but what his family had been doing for generations, growing taller (some were six-foot-six, drinking harder, while their land holdings grew smaller). Among the parents and the grandparents models for personhood were limited.

However, the one notable thing my great-great-grandfather Butt had done was to marry a Roman Catholic girl named Honora Hurley, whose own birthdate is merely a question mark on my father's family tree. But in marrying her on a cold December day in 1831, Robert Butt did my grandmother and me the favour of giving us an ancestress to conjure with, a Celt who was everything my stern puritan folk were not. I like to imagine that she had red hair and strong arms and a stride that tamed opposition. She had come off the boat in St. John's at the age of twelve because, although her family was bound from Cork to New York, her father couldn't take the ocean for one more league. So they became Newfoundlanders. She met her husband on the Labrador, where the two families fished together. They had a most unusual marriage agreement: all sons would be Protestants, all daughters Catholics. I imagine both churches disapproved, but Honora kept her religion and her bargain with her husband as well. My father tells me that while his mother lived with us in her last years she began to talk a lot about her grandmother, "Aunt Honor."

I must have heard these stories. Maybe even while I washed that kitchen floor badly I was hearing about "Aunt Honor" and her feats. She was called "Aunt" because in Newfoundland that was the honorary title given to all older women, but especially to those who make themselves indispensable to the community. In those days there were no hospitals to deliver babies or to care for the sick and dying, no social workers to find homes for the orphans or mediate family fights, no psychiatrists to give solace and guidance to those who were addled. These things were done by women. They were done by my great-great-grandmother Aunt Honor. The fact that she was a Catholic coming into a family of Methodists didn't compromise her charity. Twenty summers spent hauling children back and forth to the Labrador fishery didn't wear her out. Even though her class was set by her husband coming from the wrong side of the harbour and being a drunk to boot, she was not intimidated in her work as community resource.

So I like to believe that Ann, child of the drunk and the weak, made herself in her grandmother's image, the strong woman, ministering to family and community. But she wasn't quite as pure as Honora, not quite so unstinting, not quite so generous in her love of her fellow humankind. After all, she was not a Catholic and had no Virgin Mary as an example of sacrificial womanhood. Ann was a Protestant and she had what we would call today an attitude problem. My father says she was not a joiner, so although she would offer individual charity in the form of food from her garden, she could not be a modest enough woman to always bow to the church and become a church lady of charity. As well, her charity tended to be accompanied by lectures to the recipients, about how to successfully get their own daily bread. She took in her prematurely senile mother and her reformed father, policed the mother's attempts to throw the children down the well, while not undermining her father's reform with reminders of past sins. She taught her illiterate husband how to read and she made her sons and daughters into hard-working, literate adults, but it made her a hard task-mistress and finally she became, in her attitude to mortals if not to her God, what my father calls a "cynic."

What brings a woman to that subject position most discouraged for women, cynicism? I think being Honora's grandchild must have helped. You see it strikes me that she must have wondered, when she was very young, how come Aunt Honor, her own amazing grandmother, could save and nurture and protect whole communities, but could not keep her own son from beating his wife and children? Maybe because Aunt Honor was an impostor too, like me. There she was, trying to convince all those Protestants that she lived with that a Roman Catholic was not the devil's own tool, taking on duties that would break an ordinary person in order to prove her goodness. But as powerful as she must have looked to her granddaughter, she was not powerful. She did not have authority. Her own husband, if he so desired, could walk up to her at any time and smash her face in and it would not be punished. Any church official could condemn her and her ecumenical arrangement concerning her children and her work would count as nothing and anyone she nursed or midwifed could refuse to pay, and that would be that. Of course her goodness was mostly appreciated and people did pay when they could, and the churches, both her husband's and her own, tolerated her and we do not know about her husband and his potential for violence. We only know she had a violent son.

Her granddaughter Ann, being a smart little girl, must have also seen that at the heart of things Honora's moral superiority held no sway, at the heart of things she was an impostor, a woman who allowed little girls to believe she had the power to make things right, but when Ann most needed her she was not there. When the floorboards felt the heavy boots of the father and brothers returning drunk, knocking over the table, the stove, anything in their way, and the mother came into bed with Ann and her sister, hushing them, the three of them huddling, hoping tonight that unconsciousness rather than anger would be the result of the drink, it must have occurred to the bright little girl that her grandmother, Honora, did not have the power of the mantle she wore in the community. I like to think that Ann figured out what all the great male thinkers of her time and ours have failed to understand: their solutions for human woes are riddled with hypocrisy since their prescriptions continue to assume that women's unpaid work will be done and that, as a rule, women need no effective defence against male violence. Neither Honora nor Ann had the power to save those that most needed them.

And neither does good Queen Lillibet, and neither do I. That's the hard part of being our fathers' daughters, being daddies' girls. Doing your duty, doing ten times your duty will never really get you the power to change the culture of the fathers that we have inherited. Despite the fact that my grandmother had a "good" husband, as I do, despite the fact that she loved her aged reformed father as I love mine, she silently never forgave his violence, as I have never accepted that it was right for my father to go away to war and then to go away again to peace. I understand the patriarchy we have to live in; I even understand how it also makes victims of men. But I do not forgive it. My grandmother became a cynic when she was old, and I find each day that goes by it is harder and harder not to resort to cynicism. Lillibet must find it so too. She must sometimes resent the fact that the empire she inherited, like the one many daddies' girls are inheriting today, is no empire, but a battered, hungry and angry child. Despite all the mantles we put on to go about our daily work, the cynicism occasionally shows through like a frayed seam. I remember when the Queen made that speech in the London guildhall after her children had shamed her with their public affairs and broken marriages. She said, with a fine British understatement, that it had been a hard year. It takes a cynic to make such a joke.

One of the ways I notice my own cynicism emerging is the way I treat the traditional holidays. It is Christmas soon, and I have deliberately avoided seeking to have any of my family with me here in Florida. I went to see them in November, so there would be no good reason to join them for Christmas. Christmas makes me cynical. The problem with cynicism is that it is really only a crusty scab covering a wound. One scratch will start it bleeding again. A few hours with family on the blessed day might well do the trick, reminding you of all the ways in which the family is not holy, is not whole. I used to work very hard year after year to make Christmas Days pleasant for my children, and I like to think mostly they were. To put me in the right mood, I would stay up late on Christmas Eve after all the presents were put out and listen to Handel's *Messiah* and sip on scotch. When I got a good buzz on the music would bring back to me, temporarily, the vision of that powerful male force that was supposed to make my childhood safe. Last year I didn't play the tape and I have to be careful with the scotch as my body ages. This year I did not bring Handel with me to Florida, and I have promised myself to turn off all television hallelujah choruses. You see, I'm trying to make my peace with my idea of my father, and the way that idea has betrayed me. I think it might help me feel less like an impostor in my writing and begin to let that very unfeminine cynicism show. Let the scabs open to the air. Let them heal.

And meanwhile I still ask my dad to tell me about his mom. Mostly I learn nothing new, but sometimes he lets drop a pearl, like the fact that his mother never told him of her troubled childhood until after she had "lost her mind" in her old age. As I write I too feel like I am losing my mind, my daddy's-girl mind.

Recently, my father verified my uncle Rich's story of Nanny Clarke believing in fairies. He tells me that once in her fifties, when she was about my age, she was out berry-picking with my uncle Rich. She started to head away from him, not picking any more, just walking briskly ahead in a straight line away from the road, from home, from safety, walking as if she knew where she was going. He called her, loudly, several times before she turned and gradually came back to him. "The fairies took me," she said, "but your voice called me back."

The fairies take me every now and then as I age, and I am trying hard not to let the voices of men call me back. One of the ways I do this is to refuse to read too many men's books. Of course I must sometimes, just to keep my job, but mostly I try to read the books of women, especially women who write of their own lives. A memoirist I admire, Maxine Hong Kingston, says that her father owns a Chinese translation of her memoirs in which there are large margins allowing for the Chinese tradition of commentary. When she saw her father's beautifully written ideographs in the margins of her book she was so touched that she placed the copy in a library exhibit of her works and took him there to see it. He pointed the text out to those around him and announced that this was "my writing." I have sent copies of some of the things I have written to my father. There is no commentary. In the memoir I imagined in my head there were wide spaces between the lines, spaces that my father might have written in, tracing his commentary, his story in the lines between mine, as I have written my life between the lines of his. That kind of man's story I would like to read. With that idea of fatherhood I could make my peace.

Avalon: Knowing My Place

I come from a place called Avalon, the Avalon Peninsula in Newfoundland, and there was a time when I liked to conjure with the history of that name. In my thirties, when I was discovering the ancient stories of the goddess, I used to play with the idea of Avalon as the place where the priestesses came from in the Arthurian legends, the misty place they returned to when they lost their battles with the kingdoms of men. When men named the Avalon Peninsula of Newfoundland they were probably not thinking of priestesses. Perhaps, after so long and hard a journey, they thought they were arriving at Avalon, the place of the dead, or on a fine day with the capes lit up by the western sun, perhaps they thought they had come to paradise, the Isle of Avalon. Yet, there are many days when they might see an Avalon that brought the ancient women to mind, a land of fog and sharp rocks with headlands waiting to trap the weary sailor, a place men dreaded, as the Arthurian tradition dreads the females of ancient Avalon, makes them the supernatural enemies of men.

When I was little I imagined the Avalon Peninsula quite differently from what I know it to be today. Since I was too young for a proper education in history or geography, I imagined the places of Avalon from my own small experience of travelling with my family from St. John's around the arc of Conception Bay to Carbonear and Victoria, the home towns of my parents, and from hearing adults around me speaking of the comings and goings of other adults, of their days and ways in the hundreds of settlements along the peninsula's shorelines. Thus, Avalon grew in my head, not neatly dividing into four peninsulas of land—peninsulas within a peninsula—as it is today on my road map, but rather four bays of the sea, great bodies of water with small luminous crescents of land etching the vast blue-green ocean. Each crescent had place names—Placentia, St. Mary's, Trinity, Conception—that conjured up a child's history of my homeland, my family and myself.

Placentia Bay seemed so far away, its story so distant from my own family's, that it might have been a foreign land. Indeed it had been. It was where the enemy, the French, had held sway, and as far as I knew, lived there still. In my child's mind the world of Placentia and its foreign past was as far away as France where the soldiers had died in the last war and were still dying in the new war. As an adult I drove the short distance from St. John's to Placentia with Richard, to the fort high on the cliffs above the town, and there we found those cartoon-type cutouts of eighteenth-century French soldiers and put our heads in the spaces where faces should be and then took each other's snapshots. Although the fortress at Placentia is a national park, I noticed that the descriptions of the French and their activities printed on those careful little informational signs that national parks supply were not exactly in the usual Parks Canada style; the language of these signs still held enough of the dread of the Newfoundland heart for the French fact in its history to give the descriptions a virulence not common in the omniscient neutrality of government-approved issue.

St. Mary's Bay, although only a few hours travel for us tourists in this day, could have been on the moon in my childhood, for no one I had ever heard of lived there, no adult I knew ever went there. Its very name made me think of Roman Catholics who worshipped Mary. Or so I was told. Nobody ever said why that was an evil thing, but I could tell by the tone of voice that any such pagan practice as worshipping a mere mother certainly was not to be tolerated by us Protestants. So naming a bay Mary could only be bad.

Trinity Bay seemed to my young ears a pleasant place to come from not only because we pledged our faith in the Holy Trinity when we went to church, but also because Trinity Bay was rimmed with places like Heart's Delight, Heart's Desire, Heart's Content, and Little Heart's Ease. The only person I had ever met from these places was a young woman who had come to help my mother with housework and was as good as her origins. Orpha was a delight to me in her easygoing humour and warm physicality which brought with her a daily tolerance of the accidents of real life, everything from the no-commentary wipe-up of spilled milk to the easy settlement of the battles of children through routine separation of combatants with no comments on the nature of the disagreement.

This was not something that we were used to. I lived in a very rational world where personal responsibility was involved in all events, a cause and effect world where the words "spilling" and "wasting" were equivalent so that milk accidentally tipped from my glass was met with "you've wasted your milk." Fresh milk was an expensive and precious commodity on the rocky Avalon, and unless I could find a way to blame it on someone else, I must take the responsibility and examine my character for a milk-wasting fault. Orpha would merely wipe the milk up with a grin and a tease: "Look now, my lover, put your glass farther from that busy elbow." I longed to live in Heart's Content or Heart's Delight, believing that there no one would find evidence of a tendency to laziness in my habit of staring out windows, and my ability to trip over nothing and drop everything would not be interpreted as a willful illness. In Heart's Desire and Little Heart's Ease I was sure that little girls spilled tons of milk and none of it was wasted. In my imagination, in my desire, Trinity Bay lapped like an ocean of milk around a world of fulfilled desires and flowed into bays of contentment ebbing away into the heart's own ease.

Not all places on the rims of the bays of the Avalon of my pre-geography experience were as kindly. There was one Avalon area of terrifying and continually attractive mystery. The mystery began one day when I was in our backyard on Craigmillar Avenue watching my father put little paper caps over the early cabbage plants to protect them from spring frosts. The southern view, from anywhere in old St. John's, is dominated by the ridge of the South Side Hill. It seemed impossible to me that anyone could go to the top of that hill, let alone go beyond it. These were the days before the hill became crisscrossed with freeways and housing developments and a child could still imagine such impossibilities.

"What is over the South Side Hill?" I asked my father. "Ferryland" was his one word answer to my years of wondering about the mystery of beyond the South Side Hill. My father was a factual man and busy with his cabbages.

Now my dad had said "Ferryland," however, for the next several years, I believed that there was a place called "Fairyland" which became the locus of my fictions of the supernatural. Whenever wicked or benign forces came my way, such as the mummers at our door at

Christmas time, whenever a whiff of "little people" entered my brain from the stories of old-timers who believed in such entities, whenever the convincing reality of ghosts spilled out from that small crack of darkness where my parents had failed to tightly close the closet under the eves of my bedroom, I conjured up the large bulk of the South Side Hill and planted it firmly across the circle of my inner skull. Beyond the hill, stretching endlessly across a landscape both beautiful and terrifying, was "Fairyland."

The feeling of the otherness of the South Side Hill and beyond was especially powerful because before you could even get to the hill, you had to cross Topsail Road, travel the paths of the Protestant cemetery, a place full of graves as old as St. John's; you had to dare the traffic of Waterford Bridge Road, and walk the bridge over the Waterford River. As if all these things were not impediment enough to one of my years, before I got to the first steep scramble up the side of the hill, I had to cross the railroad tracks, resisting the temptation to put a penny on the tracks as the older boys did, since I had been told that doing so could derail a train. I imagined the cars leaping from the tracks, bouncing indiscriminately into houses, river, cemetery, the graves opening, and then.... It was all too horrible. Better to put the ridge of the South Side Hill across the vision in my head, and send the thought over the edge into "Fairyland."

When I was very young, perhaps no more than six, I was allowed to go over the Waterford Bridge to the South Side Hill to visit my Auntie Jean, mother's sister, who, while Uncle Tom was at sea, briefly lived there with her children in one of the scattered homes built on the lower part of the hill. Somehow their presence in an actual house, with dishes and furniture and a radio seemed all wrong for the South Side Hill, and I was relieved when they moved back to Carbonear, leaving me to imagine that the few houses on our part of the hill belonged to strange creatures, ones who had special powers to communicate with those beyond the ridge of the hill.

The mystery of the South Side Hill was as different as night is to day when compared to riding the old highway to Carbonear and Victoria village. That was the one crescent of the Avalon that I knew well, for at the end of that road which arched around every harbour of the bay called Conception were my parents childhood homes. Going "around the bay" was a family affair. We travelled regularly to visit our maternal grandmother, Mom Osmond, sometimes by taxi-bus or train, but most memorably in my Uncle Charl and Aunt Helen's car, with my two male cousins, who could be counted on—with my two brothers, David and Hal—to cramp my style. How could four adults and five children fit in one car? I think it was arranged like this: the two men in the front with the two older boys, one in my dad's lap, one squashed in behind the gear shift, while in the back would be the two sisters, Helen and Kathleen, and the writhing, scrapping, "It's my turn to be beside the window," bodies of the two younger boys and me. There were regular stops to accommodate children being stomach-sick from the experience of spending what seemed like interminable hours staring at the back of a car seat while the road undulated over every curve of every harbour and beach along that rocky shore.

When we visited Newfoundland a couple of years ago, the cousin whom I had shared that back seat with took Richard and me around the bay by the new road. It was an easy drive, just an hour, since it does not go "around" the bay anymore. One is offered a selection of exits from the straight-throughness of the Trans-Canada Highway, arriving at the chosen destination with none of the nonsense of "aroundness." In those slower days of going "around the bay" I can remember my mother whispering regularly in my ear, "Helen, you tell us when you are going to get sick; don't try to hold it." But when I would tell her, it would always be in a place too narrow to stop and I would have to try to hold it. Sometimes I couldn't. Then the cry of the boys beside me, "Helen's being sick. She's being sick right now!" would send the car careening off into some narrow roadside place and I would be hauled out to the side of the road, the vomit dripping through my fingers as I went.

Now I remember not the vomit as much as the views. In the car I rarely saw the places we travelled through, since looking out the side windows only increased the likelihood of motion sickness. The only alternative was to jostle with the boys for a view over the front seat, between the shoulders of the men and over the heads of the older boys. This led to much jockeying for position, trod-on toes and tender ribs from territorial elbows. Eventually I would give up and cry on my mother's lap or stare grumpily at the back of the front seat, flipping open and shut the little ashtray in its middle, until my mother would pull my hands away and make me stop. So when I got out of the car to vomit, the sight of a rock face, the sweep of a pebbly beach or even someone's cow behind a picket fence, seemed beautiful beyond words, making my memories of that trip around Conception Bay a series of glimpses of landscape filled with the vivid release of my body from its malaise.

On some of these occasions I must have been taken into the front seat after vomiting, resulting in the banning of my older brother or my cousin to the back, for I can remember the accusations of both of them, casting me into the shame of "sissy." "You sissy. Did it on purpose to get in the front." Taking one of their places meant being squeezed up against Uncle Charl, who told funny jokes, or between my father's knees where I could occasionally leap up and see the open road before the movement of the car pressed me down again. This was a place of honour worth the throwing up.

The really good part of these crowded car trips was the fact that it took so long to go to Carbonear by the winding seaside route that we had to stop for a "boil-up" along the way. As the halfway point would approach, the adults would begin to discuss the virtues of various stopping places for the purpose of boiling the kettle for tea and a meal, urged on by us kids who would have begun, after the first ten miles, to be hungry and complain that it was taking forever. I can remember being told by my father before we left home in the morning—after my mother had whispered to him, "you warn Helen, she won't listen to me"—that I was not to annoy our generous uncle by constantly asking when we would be stopping for our boil-up. It seems I was the most vocal complainer and I had better learn my place as guest in the back seat of my uncle's car. So I would try hard not to start the complaint, but once the cry of hunger was initiated by one of the other children, I joined in with enthusiasm, an enthusiasm that made my voice more noisy to adults than the voices of boys. When the parents finally chose the beach, or meadow or roadside scrap of flat land on which the boil-up would happen, we would tumble out and despite the calls of "don't go too far; don't go where we can't see you" we would be off as far and as fast as we could go. I can't remember ever playing with any of those boys with whom I kept such intimate company in my uncle's car, so glad I was to be away from their elbows and knees and feet.

Perhaps that's where my habit of going off by myself began, for now I recall that the whole imaginative geography of my girlhood was discovered while I was alone, such as on those walks taken to get away from boys, to get away from being my mother's child. On those rides to Carbonear, when the tea kettle was boiled over the open fire, and the sandwiches and bowls of potato salad, the devilled eggs and jars of pickles were laid out on a tablecloth, when the boys had long ago wolfed down their drinks and food and run off to another game, my mother would still be calling me to come to eat: "You were so hungry before we stopped and now you'll have to eat so fast you'll make yourself sick again."

Writing these words of the places of my childhood has led to two days during which I could not write anymore, during which the Florida sunshine that has encouraged this writing declined into a thin winter fog, neither warm nor really cool and two days in which the fog of depression descended over me. Attempting to break it by doing some Christmas shopping in this frost-free land has only made it worse, making me realize once more how I isolate myself to marginality and loneliness by the very choices I make to give myself space to exist. I came to this place away from the climate and the people I am used to in order to write. And being here I find myself too much alone. Writing has become like getting out of the car for a boil-up. I yearn and yearn to be away from the tight squeeze of bodies, the constant assault of the nausea of the careening ride, then rushing into the fresh air and across the strand of beach or through the low pines of a rocky hillside, I find myself suddenly alone, bereft of everything and everybody that makes me.

At this moment I have one of those sudden images that the mind cannot name as memory or imagination. I am off on one of my escape walks along a beach of my childhood. I find a beach rock that is white and speckled like an egg from some great prehistoric bird, an ancient child left to warm in the sun. I am so enamoured of this rock that I carry it, with great difficulty, for it is too large for my small arms, back to where my mother sits on the beach, talking with my aunt. I keep trying to interrupt them to show my rock, but they put me off, shut me out, so busy they are with being sisters. Finally, in exhaustion, I sit silently beside my mother. As I feel the warmth of her leg through the soft fabric of her full skirt, my eyes scan the beach. I realize that the beach rock I have brought from so far away is exactly like all the other rocks around us. The whole half circle of the beach is completely covered with rocks worn smooth as eggs by the millions of years of the sea. I am devastated with embarrassment.

As a child I believed that each discovery I made was the first and greatest ever made. When I grew old enough to know that the only newness in my discovery was the fact that I had made it, the redness that spread all over my skin went so deep that I felt the hotness in my arteries, the burning in my heart. As an adult I have also felt the same childhood feeling of being devastated by embarrassment, never having fully lost the naïveté of believing in the uniqueness of my discoveries. I have merely learned to cover it a little, painfully understanding that part of growing up is, after all, learning the insincerity of modesty. Sometimes I am incapable of insincerity and I let it show that I think I have just made a remarkable discovery. In my part of the world, academia, you can be sure someone always corrects my ignorance, and the embarrassment spreads again through my arteries. That day, on the beach of my childhood, my embarrassment was multiplied by every rock on the beach. I had tried to make myself special, call attention to myself by showing these women something they could see all around them. Thank goodness they were too busy to look. What would I have done if they had noticed me, heard me exclaiming over my very special rock? How they would have laughed! Sitting there, I was devastated by my own stupidity, my own ridiculous assumption that I had something that anyone would want to see, to hear about.

That feeling of worthlessness has come again in these last two days. After my writing sorties into my childhood, after my rambles on this Florida beach, these memoirs seem nothing more than common stories that lie all around to be seen by everyone. I will need to find the eccentric conviction that Richard has about the shells he collects from the beach. He goes each day for long strolls at low tide, arriving back with small treasures: sea plants, shells, strange objects shaped by sand and sea and sun. He bathes them in bleach, or boils them in vinegar and water, sorts them, assembles them, puts them in containers. We will take them home when we leave, for what purpose no one knows. Yesterday I scolded him, trying to get him to pack them up faster, for my parents arrive soon, and his shells, if they are still about the place, will not please my mother: What are they for? Why does he collect them? When will they be gone? There is no place here for his shells.

Why, when I am trying to write of the places of my childhood, do I think of my husband and his shells? I think it has to do with there being no place in the house of my childhood for things that did not serve a useful purpose. I remember a time in my late thirties when my mother and father visited us, when Richard and I still lived in our home in Winnipeg, the house we lived in the longest, where we raised our children to adulthood. My mother was sitting in the living room with me, mending something for one of the children. She confessed that she had asked father just that morning if he could live the way we did, and he agreed it would be difficult.

"What way?" I asked.

"With so many things around. Books and nicknacks, plants everywhere, things all over the coffee tables and mantlepiece." Mother didn't know how hard I worked to keep order in our home, how I gleaned through the books and magazines that everyone else seemed to want to keep around forever to see which ones I could safely store or discard, how I rearranged the potted greenery to make them look less crowded, how I sometimes pruned the plants and threw things out when my husband and children were not looking. I had worked particularly hard to get things orderly before my parents came. The place was actually looking quite good. The room they were sleeping in had been a particular challenge, the place where the family watched television being a centre for clutter and dirt. It was now spotless.

In my childhood home clutter kept catching up with my mother, as it later would with me as I gradually developed the housewife's mind that reaches outward from her body to find the rooms that enclose her are reflections of the cluttering of her mind with the activities of others. The housewife's mind cannot be uncluttered without destroying living, breathing beings, so she works hard at some order in the rooms around her, for sanity's sake. When I was a child, walking away as my mother tidied the house had always brought both an escape and a guilty loneliness as I avoided the weight of women's work. Later, as a mother myself, I managed temporary escapes into the public workplace and into the long walks that are what are left of my childhood wanderings.

These jaunts came after the world had failed to please or be pleased by me. To be included in the games of other children both thrilled me and left me feeling frightened at the nearness, the incessant demands of belonging. I would go often to the home of my friend Eleanor, who had many dolls, unbroken tea sets and a verandah wide enough to make several houses in our imaginations. We would spend hours changing the dolls' clothing, laying out the tea sets and putting them away, making up stories about the dolls, of how they belonged to families of many sisters. Eleanor and I had no sisters, were surrounded by brothers and grew up in a time when all girls of the middle classes read *Little Women*. I felt deprived of sisters. When I did finally get a sister she turned out to be a baby who had to be wheeled around in a

carriage and whose presence once provoked another girl I played with
to tell me to go home: the Clarkes had too many children, she said, and
her mother had told her that you didn't have to have that many babies.
She was an only child. So I played with Eleanor who never commented
on the size of my family. But soon the intense femaleness of our play
would tire me and Eleanor's dolls were not mine, my dolls seeming to
be lost, injured or destroyed as quickly as I gained them. So off I would
go, to wander in the cemetery alone or climb as far as my small legs
could carry me, up the South Side Hill.

Twice my play with Eleanor brought crises of such major propor-
tions that I had to climb very, very high up the South Side Hill. Once
was when I stole one of her dolls. I had called on her and she was out,
probably playing with that girl next door, Marcia, an American inter-
loper whose father was an officer at "the base" and whose mother,
unlike our busy mothers, had time to comb and comb and comb Marcia's
long dark hair. Marcia and I did not like each other; we were rivals for
Eleanor. So I hung around the verandah of Eleanor's house a while,
wishing her mother (whose voice was kinder than my mother's harried
sounds) was my mother, and that she might invite me in to spend some
time in the house that seemed so much richer than my own, more like
the houses in my school readers. Time passed and I was not invited in. I
began to wonder if I should seek out the girls and throw rocks at Marcia, but finally decided to go find out what the boys were doing.

As I jumped the steps down from the verandah two at a time, there
at the side of the garden was one of Eleanor's dolls, a rag-tag one, not
her best. I did not think "I will steal Eleanor's doll," I just picked it up
and went home, as if that was something one could do ever so naturally.
Of course it wasn't. I was running within fifty feet, and since her house
was directly across from the cemetery, as was mine, I had to cover
almost the entire length of the cemetery to our house with all those
dead witnesses to accuse me. By the time I got home it was as if I had a
corpse on my hands. I do not know where I hid the doll, certainly not
inside my mother's house. My instinct told me I had to get up the steep
side of the South Side Hill as fast as I could. So across Topsail Road and
through the cemetery I rushed, despite all the bony fingers that
reached out to grab me from the soldiers and sailors and pirates buried
centuries ago. Across Waterford Bridge Road, heedless of traffic I went,
over the bridge quickly so that I would not be captured by the sound
and sight of the water which always made me want to jump from the

bridge, and up the side of the hill scrambling until I had no breath left to challenge its steepness. There I sat and cried and looked down through my tears at the tiny roofs of the houses, the winding of the streets, the movements of cars and people. I could see Eleanor's house. I could see mine. I could see my brothers playing baseball in the field near our house, and I could see my mother hanging the wash on the line in our backyard. Down Topsail Road I could see two girls skipping and figured they must be Eleanor and Marcia. I looked for signs in the clouds, hoping for some instruction from on high. None came. I knew I would have to stay up on the South Side Hill forever, never going among people again.

For I was a thief. All the stories of the outlaws I had ever read or seen at the movies assaulted me, and despite knowing the stories of Robin Hood and Billy the Kid, I could find no model for my doll snatching. I wish I could report, like St. Augustine, that my sin eventually led to God, but it did not. St. Augustine had only stolen a pear; I, despite being a devotee of *Little Women*, had stolen the doll of the good, sisterly Eleanor. Surely this was an unredeemable act, stealing your best friend's doll. Nobody would ever be able to whitewash this, no matter how much of my future ill-gotten gains I gave to the poor, no matter how many times I saved the beautiful lady on the stagecoach from the unspeakable desecrations of my fellow crooks, nothing could wipe out such a despicable act.

With my self-dramatization at full hilt, I decided that the only course of action open to me was to escape over the top of the hill into "Fairyland" and accept whatever fate awaited me there. Off I set. Steeper and steeper the hill grew, smaller and smaller became I, until finally there were trees. Now one of the nice things about living on the Avalon Peninsula was that there were not too many trees, as least not many big ones. Horizons were always available. Look one way out to sea, look another over the low brush and rock of rolling hills and there, dependable as daylight, was the sky, keeping the earth in order, making sense of up and down. Later in life I would be able to drive for thirteen hours at a stretch across the vastness of the Canadian Prairies and love it, because it felt so good to always see the distant horizon. But that day, the scrubby and short trees of the Avalon growing on the South Side Hill became suddenly as thick as the densest forest, as dark as any fairy would require to trick the mind of a small child. I lost all confidence in my escape.

Those trees did not inspire me with thoughts of wombs and maternal protection. I have never sought the claustrophobia of greenery. I need vistas to make sense of the world. So as the branches of those terrible trees began to reach out like the bony fingers of the dead in the graves below the hill, I turned and fled downwards. I was too faint-hearted to choose the exile's hermitage in the fairy woods, to become the fairy child, lost to the ordinary world, alive only to the fairy band's shenanigans and magic. And I am still faint-hearted today. I have always had to come back and find some trick to make them let me inside the gates of the village again. It is always a trick, one of subterfuge or braggadocio, but one that works for a while. This time I chose subterfuge. I retrieved the doll from its hiding place, raced with it hidden inside my jacket to Eleanor's house and tossed it among the flowers in her father's rock garden, where anyone watching from the house would not see me, but where the parents would surely find the doll and scold Eleanor for putting it there. Perhaps she would blame her brothers for trying to murder her doll and all would be normal again.

Playing with Eleanor would be more difficult after that because of the corpse that always stood between us. The distance between her and me caused by my now-criminalized mind emboldened me to go one night on an expedition to steal her father's crabapples in the company of some boys whom I was trying to impress. I could not actually bring myself to go closer than her fence, but I did watch, and therefore condone, the apple stealing. Our friendship cooled somewhat after that, until puberty, blooming in households of boys, would once more bring us close.

Eleanor and dolls were also the occasion of one more flight to the South Side Hill. When we were about ten a remarkable event occurred in the history of the technology of dolls. They started to have hair you could comb and curl. The revolutionary effect of this is hard to imagine in the present moment. Suffice it to say that it drove girls, who a few months earlier were bragging that they had outgrown dolls, back to them with a vengeance. They had the disciplining effect on our femininity that Barbie would have on the next generation of girls a decade or two later. Now that we could indulge in the grown-up activities of combing, curling and styling, we turned back to dolls with a new belief in the value of beauty. This invention of combable, curlable hair was better than dolls that drank water and peed. Such damp entities implied the drudgery of motherhood. These dolls with hair offered us the freedom every girl wants, the freedom to spend hours each day, year after year, decade after decade, for a whole lifetime, trying to make sense of her hair. Everyone who was anyone got a doll with combable hair for Christmas or birthday that year. Eleanor did and shared her good fortune with me. I did not, and shared my miserableness with my mother. Kathleen did not quite understand the revolutionary nature of the new phenomenon, and kept countering my every argument with the maddening rightness of her logic: "You said you were too old for dolls."

"But this is one with hair, with hair you can comb, Mom." I had not yet learned the imperious sarcasm of calling her "Moth-er," with a heavy emphasis on the separateness of each syllable so that the word spits into the face of the woman who once cradled you in her womb. I was, after all—despite my intractable will, my tendencies for self-dramatization, and my sometimes near-hysterical anger—only a ten-year-old child, not yet a tactical teenager. And so I went up to the hill that day with the absolute belief in the tragedy of my existence. I would never get that doll; I would grow old, a miserable unwanted unlovable woman who could never take any joy in life because I had not been given the pleasure of a doll with real hair. On the hill I looked for messages from God in the clouds moving by and saw one that looked like a duck and later another one shaped like a camel, neither of which could be signs from the Almighty. Finally I saw one shaped like Australia, a continent I had recently become aware of on a globe we had received for Christmas, and took it as a sign that dolls with hair were to remain as far from my life as the other side of the world. I came back cleansed by the isolation of my place above the world, and ready to face a life of tragedy.

Within a day my mother had bought me a doll with hair. I was flabbergasted. I had never received a present that was not for Christmas or birthday, and both days were past months since. This was unheard of. I knew, even at my age, how little my mother had in the way of discretionary cash. She made her own bread to save money, purchased cheap white margarine instead of butter and doled out the expensive supply of fresh milk each day at noon hour. Besides, there had been no sign in the clouds of anything like this. "You can thank your Aunt Helen for that," said my mother, handing me the doll. "She convinced me to buy it for you." She seemed to be trying to assure me that she was not taking any part in my corruption. Why had I seen no cloud signs? No lightning bolts presaged this great change. How could my mother tamper with my fate in this unheard-of manner? I was not meant to have this doll;

my mother did not want me to have this doll; and looking at the doll I realized that the doll did not want me.

I tried to play with the thing for a few days, combing its wretched auburn hair, sticking curlers in its stupid pageboy, and setting it up where I could see it at night to help me believe in the reality of its staring eyes framed by those stiff wisps of whatever petroleum product the hair was made from. I took the doll over to Eleanor's and she seemed really pleased to see I had at last been given my doll with hair. Other girls "Oh'd" and "ah'd", but it was no use. I had thrown dolls out of my life in that pseudo-Augustinian moment up there on the hill and I had accepted my doll-less existence. To own this thing now was to be an impostor. To play with it was to extend my impostorhood. I knew it and the doll knew too. I kept her hidden, except for occasions when girls I needed to impress came around. Showing her off made me feel like an impostor too.

Decades later, when I was in the stage I now call my "high feminist phase," my own daughter yearned for a Barbie; all her friends had Barbies. Having decided that my daughter would grow up untainted by hair and body obsessions and knowing that Barbie's body was an offence to womankind, I refused for about eight months, finally realizing, as I suppose my mother did, that a mother's resistance makes the desired object shimmer with import, a possession, a religion, a self withheld by the mother who should want this for her daughter, want it as much as she should want her daughter to be a woman who is beautiful, loved because she has real, curly hair. I gave up, as my mother did before me, not very gracefully. As the saying goes, "We are slaves and the daughters of slaves." Maybe we should revise that old feminist cliché: "We are impostors and the daughters of impostors."

Speaking of being an impostor, I spent a lot of my youth looking for a place among boys. And I've delayed writing about this problematic place of my childhood for a couple of days now, because I'm a little afraid that any way I tell it will merely multiply my impostorhood. You see, I had planned to make it into a throwaway joke, the one the comedian reels off as afterthought, vaguely, but not immediately related to the jokes that went before. I liked that idea. You would read it as if we were just having this really relaxed, casual, self-mocking conversation that people have about the foibles of their youth. Then, when I was finished you would suddenly realize its intricate and subtle connection to the theme of place and you would laugh and then applaud in admiration of my performance. This now seems to me to be just more impostor-hood, so I took a long walk on the beach to think about writing.

The year is winding down now. Even in Florida the days are darker, the birds feed with less enthusiasm, the Floridians put on sweaters and pretend its winter. As I walked I began to get my feminist dander up. I should not throw this incident away. It was no joke. It marked such significance in my life that I have never forgotten it. This was one of the handful of events that took away my faith in what I thought was real. So maybe I had better not cast it casually to you in comic understatement; maybe I had better give it some oomph, a few adjectives, a little heroism. For looking back I feel that during this childhood event I was a little heroic, as well as mad, when I threatened to kill a boy with my father's axe.

I often played with boys. I don't remember anyone remarking on this being unusual. Play was so unorganized in the world I grew up in that although it was often gendered, nobody remarked when it wasn't. What I mean to say is that nobody enrolled us in girls' ringette teams, or boys' hockey teams, girls' softball or boys' baseball. Parents could not afford either the time or money for such organized sports. We were sent daily, weather permitting, out of houses and we were expected to find other children and learn games and play them. This was not something that required supervision. Of course the school world was a gender-segregated one, and there were Brownies and Cubs, Girl Guides and Boy Scouts, but our play time was often ungendered. One of the things I liked about my childhood was the way play groups shifted and changed, groups of playmates emerging, blending, breaking, depending on the activity. I played "hoist your sails and run," "Simon says" and baseball in a field near our home with a gang of kids, mostly boys, because our street was top-heavy with boys, and I played house with a little girl from up the street and her younger brother, since both obeyed me and played my way. When I wanted more mature play, there was hopscotch and skipping, dolls and board games at Eleanor's house on Topsail Road. I had choices, and I liked that. And of course, there was always the South Side Hill.

Perhaps I was seven or eight the year we built a club in the untamed brush in the backyard next door. The club consisted of me and my older brother and the two boys next door, and the gravekeeper's son from across Topsail Road. At first I didn't notice I was the only girl. I was often the only girl and that didn't worry me. We built quite a nice clubhouse. There were planks and branches and real nails and hammers as I recall. I worked with enthusiasm as did the others. It was to be a secret club of course, with secret codes, secret passwords and secret activities. I had read the Hardy Boys and Nancy Drew books and knew about such things. I had no doubt that this was, for me, known territory, owned territory. We inaugurated the club by stealing some tea, wrapping it in brown paper and attempting to smoke it. Life was good.

When I arrived at club meeting time a day later, there was a sign nailed to the club door. Yes, those little worms had actually gone to the trouble to print the essence of their nasty little closed minds on a sign and nail it up: "No Girls Allowed." It's an old story and I'm sure you knew its climax before I told it. But perhaps its dénouement (remember the axe?) has a special twist that might be worth considering.

I recall very clearly that I was absolutely, completely and sincerely in possession of only one emotion when I saw that sign: outrage. I have spent a walk or two on the beach to make sure I am telling you no lie, that there were not more sympathetic and feminine emotions, like sadness, sorrow or shame involved in my reaction. No. I was still untouched enough by the ideology I lived in, still impervious enough to the plots of civilization in the beauty of my child's mind, still sweet enough in my since-polluted heart, to believe I belonged in that club, that the pleasure we had shared in building it was my membership card. I was outraged. Rights violated. All decency ignored. Loyalty and hard work negated. Can you even imagine a purity so lovely that could feel outrage at such an ordinary gendered act of the world we live in? I must have grown up in a place as remote as the place I imagined over the South Side Hill to even find my exclusion unusual. To feel only the dignity of outrage must have meant that I felt a sense of entitlement that nobody in their good senses would teach a female child.

But that's not the worst of it. In a most unfeminine way I decided not to cry, but to take action against a sea of foes and, by opposing, end them. I went into the basement of my father's house and I found the axe that he used to chop wood for our fireplace, and I gripped it with both my hands and I marched right out to that club house. "Kingsley," I shouted—for indeed the boy I knew must be the leader of this stupid discrimination was actually named by that significant signifier and I have no intention of changing it to protect the guilty—"Kingsley, I am going to kill you with my axe." Their high voices shrilled out, calling for their mommies. My own older brother tried reason, but I could hear the uncertainty in his voice. He knew me and although he had no experience in my handling of axes, he knew of my potential for recklessness. I stood, holding my axe high, outside the ramshackle club house, waiting for the first one that dared to exit. Unfortunately, their cries were heard by Kingsley's mother who rushed over to my mother, who came out the side door of our house.

I remember the sight and sound of my mother very clearly to this day. She came around to the back of the house, wiping her hands with her apron. She looked down to where I stood and said very distinctly, but in an unexceptional, unhurried voice, as if this situation was as common as dirty dishwater, "Helen, bring that axe home, you are not supposed to have your father's axe." Kingsley's mother sputtered about my dreadful behaviour, how something needed to be done about such a child, but my mother returned to her housework without giving the woman further satisfaction. Mother may have had to be patriarchy's policewoman, but she did not blame me for my girlchild's desire to protest its exclusivity. I returned home, put my battle-axe down among the sticks of wood where it became my father's axe again, and never spoke to Kingsley ever after. He certainly kept his distance from me.

I have only lied a little in telling you of me and my trusty axe, my desire sometimes forgetting to shape language to anything but my needs. What I have told you is all true, true as I remember it. Except for my mother's part. I do not honestly remember her words or their tone. I do not remember if she stopped to mollify the mother of Kingsley. Sometimes—out of family pride I suppose—she refused to blame us as fully as other mothers would want. I remember the time when a neighbour came from across the road and said the Clarke children were as unsupervised and rowdy as "street Arabs." Mother defended us that time. On the occasion of the axe I know for sure she was called out of the house and I know she spoke to me. I remember very distinctly having the following thought after she spoke to me: "If I kill Kingsley they will put me in jail." Was it that warning, a warning of logical consequences, that my mother gave me when she spoke? Memory fails me.

The mother I have just invented—the one whose worldly words speak of necessary compromise in the unfair world of men, but whose tone of ancient mythic wisdom does not condemn her daughter for the natural desire to cut off the heads of exclusionary men with her righteous battle-axe—that is the mother I need; the desire for her makes language invent itself in me. The words may have to stifle and smother in the throat or pander and prettify themselves in the language of men, but where they start, deep in the bowels and the guts and the womb, they are real; and when they speak, as they did that day out of the mouth of that child, the precious pearl of women's outrage, that language, those words come from a place that may be as misty as Avalon, but it is language that is still real. We deny its reality at our peril.

So that is an account of how I learned my place, outside of all the worlds that use my labour for their profit. I was more careful after that to seek out girls as companions. We built no clubhouses, preferring the sturdy branches of apple trees to sit above the passing scene, and talk philosophy and politics as young girls are known to do. Sometimes boys would come by and beg our apples, beg to join us on our branches, but we had neither apples nor branches to spare them.

But the plot doesn't end there. Forty years after our childhood friendship Eleanor and I met in Denmark where she was living at the time and I was visiting on an academic junket. I asked her to take me to see the *Little Mermaid*. The piece of sculpture is exactly the disappointment you have imagined, a little wimp on a rock, that everybody stands around gawking downward at. Eleanor, in her quiet way, said we might walk a hundred yards along the shore and see a statue she liked better. She took me to see a monument to mother Denmark. The great lady stands high above the heads of her citizens, her muscular arms holding the reins of four mighty bulls. Fountains in the shape of anthropomorphic beasts raise their streams in honour all around her. It seems the King of Sweden or God, Eleanor says it doesn't matter which, since the two lords held similar powers over the ancient Danes, told Denmark that she could only claim as much land as could be plowed in a day. Denmark, lacking technology, but having four strong, largely unoccupied sons, transformed them into bulls and carved up the fruitfulness that is Denmark by the end of the day. My Avalon had need of such women.

As it was Avalon did have Mom Osmond, my mother's mother, who had raised two sons and a brace of daughters who were my memorable aunts. Over the years she had become the respected Aunt Ollie to the many grateful mothers that she midwifed and the many children she delivered into the world, the dignity of her real name, Olivia, being too great for Carbonear. But I called her Mom Osmond, as my children call their maternal grandmother Mom Clarke. Every summer my mother sent me away from St. John's to visit her mother for a few weeks and it is there I received my most important lesson in knowing my place.

To this day those weeks live in me as a vividly different world. On one remarkable occasion I went alone on the railroad train. Mother had taken me once before so I knew the ropes, knew how to give my ticket to the conductor, how to use the little washroom, flushing the pee onto the galloping tracks below, and I knew how to go out on the platform behind the last car and watch where I had been. I think the fear and pleasure of travelling alone as a child should not be missed. I remember my youngest son once telling me that when we sent him to see Mom Clarke when he was quite young, the airplane was over Lake Superior so long that he thought the pilot had made an error, turning left out of Winnipeg and heading over Hudson Bay. What other body of water could be so big? I know how he felt. There are so many things that can go wrong when your parents are not with you. As my son has told me, the hardest thing is deciding to keep silent when you think something is wrong. Knowing you are a mere child and no one will heed you, fearing that if you point out some awful thing they will have a typical adult explanation and you will appear ridiculous. Yet hearing or seeing things that you know mean doom, is only part of the thrill of travelling alone. The other part is being able to move such a great distance from your mother, able to open your little lunch she has packed for you whenever you wish to open it, able to eat it in exactly the order you wish, able to stare at other people without being told you are rude, able to refuse to speak to strangers instead of giving the polite answers to questions that mothers in that day coached you in.

I suppose the situation is different now, that children, being taught to avoid conversation with strangers, must take their lives in their hands and actually speak to strangers, defying their mothers warnings. I remember so many painful occasions when parents urged me to speak to people I did not know, answer ridiculous questions about my school-work, my age, the colour of my coat, perfectly obvious things. I remember that when I travelled alone on that train, I refused to speak to anyone, especially the conductor, who wanted to make me feel at home. The last thing I wanted to feel, on this glorious adventure into alone-ness, was at home. So I spent most of the trip out on the back platform of the last car, enjoying the delicious terror of the car swaying back and forth, forcing me to hold the handrail, pay attention to my feet, shifting as nimbly as I could to stay on them, watching the world I had not yet seen recede behind me down the long perspective of the track. I remember one joyous moment when we came around a bend at Holyrood and the circling rim of Conception Bay stretched ahead, the water blue-green, the sky bright blue and the small line of clouds in the distance as pure a white as my memory can make them. Then I was happy. For that moment on my swaying deck, I was captain of my ship, maker of my destiny, so absolutely glad to be feeling no one else's feelings other than my own, wanting no one else's approval but my own. The conductor found me in this state of grace and insisted I sit inside.

That night I cried in my bed for my mother. One year I cried so much at night for my mother, that Mom Osmond sent me home. I remember when I arrived in our kitchen on Craigmillar Avenue Kathleen asked me why I had wanted to come home. I said nothing. She said no more. I looked at her—busy at her usual chores in the kitchen, moving from the floury bread-making in the pantry, to checking the stove in the kitchen—and tried to remember why I had cried to come home. Her question seemed a reasonable one and my panics in the night embarrassed me sitting there in my mother's kitchen. Suddenly she seemed like a stranger, a rather distant woman, as unconcerned with me as I was with her. Who had I cried for in the night?

But most of the times I visited Carbonear, I survived the realization of individuality, and enjoyed being there. Despite the boys who called me "townie" the place had its pleasures. Mom Osmond was an excellent cook, and Auntie Jean and my cousins seemed to me much more carefree and full of fun than my own family. Uncle Tom was often away at sea, but that was normal in Newfoundland families. My male cousin sometimes teased his older sister and me when we played "copy," as playing house was called in Carbonear and even sometimes kicked aside the stones that designated the walls of rooms of our play houses, but that was normal too. I was used to dealing with younger brothers. You ignored them, and if they got too rascally you called them mean names and then when they told their mothers you said they had started it and you had not called them anything. Afterwards, you would call them little worms for tattling to the grownups.

In the early days when I visited my cousins, before their parents built the new house, when they still all lived in the house in which my grandmother raised her many daughters, there was no running water and we had to go to the community well. Each child took a turn during the day, slinging the "square" over her shoulder, two pails in hand and running down the lane with the voice of Auntie Jean or Mom Osmond behind you telling you not to come back so fast that you spilled half the water. That was, in fact, a problem. Once you had pumped the pump enough times to fill the two pails you had to space them properly, a few feet apart, in order that the square of wood could be set down exactly at their centres with the handles of the pails on the outside of the square, so that when you lifted the handles the square caught them and balanced their weight equally. The distance thus afforded kept your arms spread wide, allowing you to bear the heaviness of the water and not be splashed. If you walked at a good steady pace, ideally you avoided losing any water. Auntie Jean was satisfied if we children managed to arrive home with the pails half full. Sometimes my pails were near empty despite the help of the device of the square.

I envied the expertise of children younger than me, and worked hard each year to regain the skill. When you had it right the feeling was lovely, your arms spreading, the force of the downward drag of water pails entirely offset by the leverage of the square pressing against the handles, freeing you so that sometimes you felt you could dance home. But it was not, in fact, so magical. Success—that is, not spilling water and being laughed at and called a townie by the children of the Back Lane in Carbonear—depended on being aware of everything, the balance of the pails against wood, the pace of walking, not too slow so that you began to jerk up and down, not too fast so that you swayed and spilled, just the right movement and stillness of legs, hips, chest, head, like a long-distance walker who must not move her arms. If you did it just right and put a nonchalant look on your face as if you weren't even concentrating, it became art, an art that got the water pails home full. But all art is site-specific and is art only because it is essential to its place and time. Soon the twentieth century would arrive, fifty years late in Carbonear, and my aunt would have a new house, one with running water and one not quite big enough to accommodate girls from the city.

But while I went to my grandmother's home, it was a place that both estranged me from myself and made me more myself. A small anecdote will do to illustrate before I leave this place of my childhood. I discovered that a girl I played with was a Catholic. Playing with Catholics was not completely unknown in my childhood. Although we went to separate schools I had cousins who were Catholic because my Auntie Thelma had "turned," as they used to say in Newfoundland, when she married her Catholic husband, Uncle John. But even though I had spent overnights with my cousins and knew them to be good pals, and understood that their brothers were no different from my brothers

as brothers go, yet, in some important part of my separate school brain,
I believed that Catholics were very different from me. Even Eleanor,
who was an Anglican and went to an Anglican school had an aura of difference. But not like Catholics. Anglicans were privileged; they weren't
really different, just more upper-class; the Queen went to their church.
Catholics, on the other hand, were not about class; they were about
what was sin and what was not.

I remember being told when using a pair of scissors on a Sunday,
that only Catholics sewed on Sunday. I was in Grace Hospital at the time,
having had my appendix out and the lady in the next bed was quite certain that my soul was in peril. I tried to tell her I was only cutting out
paper-dolls' clothing, not really sewing on the Sabbath, but there were no
exceptions: only Catholics could pick up scissors on Sundays. They could
sew, they could play cards, why they could even go skating on a Sunday.
What bliss. It had something to do with going to confession on Saturday
and then taking communion on Sunday, getting this kind of double
whammy of purity. My mother, choosing her words, told me I could cut
paper-dolls' clothing on a Sunday, but not in front of older Protestant
ladies. It was also carefully explained to me by my mother that the
Catholics were mistaken in their belief that it was all right to carry out
various activities on Sunday, especially card playing. Would they be punished then by God? She was not sure, because being mistaken was not the
same as committing a deliberate sin. Therefore, it was explained, I could
not emulate them. I knew better, therefore I must do better.

Well, this other girl and I began to discuss these fine theological
points while playing copy in the grassy lane beside my grandmother's
house. She reckoned that it was all right that she could skate on Sundays, since she was a Catholic, but she didn't see that it mattered if I
broke the Protestant rules, since I was damned to hell anyway, not
being a member of the one true church. I assured her that I said the
Apostles' Creed every Sunday at Sunday school, and in it we pledged
our allegiance to the "holy catholic church," which was the one "true"
church. I took pains to explain to her that this was not her Catholic
church, with a capital C, but another catholic church with a small c. I
knew of what I spoke because I had asked in Sunday school, and I had
been told that the word catholic with a small c meant universal, the
universal Christian church which included everyone, even Roman
Catholics, everyone, that is, except the three-quarters of the world's
population who were essentially pagans. The girl offered the opinion

that I had been taught wrongly, that from what she had been told I was damned to hell.

This refusal of rational argument and this stubborn insistence from a devotee of a religion that didn't even make its children go to Sunday school enraged me and suddenly I found a whole festering carbuncle of anti-Catholicism in my formerly ecumenical soul. I told her that Catholics were the real sinners because they thought some stupid little sentences said by a priest after some phony words of confession could lift the burden of sin we Protestants carried so nobly. I remember I had given this burden of sin some thought and realized that since my burden would get heavier each year, I had to be more careful about adding to it because I could not lay it down each week in the privacy of the confessional. As our argument heated up, I thought of a great idea. Since she had opened the discussion of hell I dared her to describe that dreadful place, so I would know exactly where I was going. At first she was unable, but with some help from my well-placed questions and hints of elaborating details, between us we were able to recount the flames and pain and darkness awaiting the sinner. After we finished I told her triumphantly that it was she and not I who was going to that terrible place, since Catholics were the biggest sinners in the world. I knew my theology was now on shaky ground, beginning to descend to invective, so I flounced away to my grandmother's house.

Next day, the proverbial all hell broke loose. It seems the girl had terrible nightmares about hellfire swallowing her up and had confessed to her mother that I had told her that all Catholics were going straight to hell. The mother came to Mom Osmond who came to me—angry in a way I had never seen her, in a way that my mother cannot quite believe today even though I have sworn its truth. My grandmother questioned me and I spilled the whole story. She gave me some whacks on my bum, lectured me about learning my proper place in the world and sent me to bed without supper.

I had plenty of time that dark night to contemplate the nature of my violation. I was pulled between several emotions. One was the sense of injustice. I had tried to tell my grandmother that the other girl had said as bad as I had, that all Protestants would go to hell, but Mom Osmond's only reply was that because I was a Protestant, I was supposed to know better, be better. It was not my place to cruelly upset little girls who were not as smart as me—and who were Catholics and never learned to argue as I did—by telling them they were doomed. To my mind this meant I was not to let Catholics know of their imminent danger, let them go on their merry way to eternal damnation. Another emotion I felt as intensely as my sense of injustice and my intellectual confusion was a commingling of shock and shame, shame that my cousins and Auntie Jean had witnessed my comeuppance, shock that my maternal grandmother (who, according to my mother was a saint who would never hit a child), had hit me. This meant either that my mother was wrong, or that I was the one child who could make Mom Osmond step down from sainthood to mortal level. To this day I have not decided which of these possibilities is the true one. However, I would point out that the Osmonds were known as "proud," and although Mom Osmond was so humble that she never took communion—feeling not worthy enough—she had married an Osmond and maybe some of the essence of being "proud" had worn off on her, and I had somehow behaved in a way inappropriate to her rank in society. Whatever the case was, she certainly did not tolerate a granddaughter who was as prideful as me.

As well as shame there was also a certain pleasurable feeling mixed with my misery. I did not know what to call it then, but since I've become a feminist and learned that language is at the heart of the great evil that has the world in its thrall, I know now that what I was enjoying in my lonely bed, when the rest of the family went for their evening walk down the Back Lane of Carbonear, was the pleasure of power in language. My words, and the words that I had drawn out of that little girl in making her describe hell, combined with the way I had then brilliantly (I thought) turned her words against her, gave me the experience of power, pure and simple. I had learned how to steal language, how to make the very language spoken to enslave me, turn on its speaker. Of course it was an abuse of power. That little girl was only the small subject of a great empire the extent of which neither of us could imagine and that empire lived within me as well. The real trick would be to learn the language of that empire so well that I could begin to make it speak its own destruction. But I didn't know that then. It takes a long time, if you are a woman, to realize you can work at having this very special subversive power to turn men's language on its makers. It takes much longer to learn that what you do with this power matters vitally, and to use it properly you must constantly short-circuit the training that makes you use it against other females or against males who have become the victims of patriarchy. It takes a whole change of self, a change in which every molecule of yourself must mutate, painfully, heartbreakingly, and completely, before you learn that you have power in language and that you can use that power for good or evil in the world. Neither the church that little girl went to nor the one I went to were appropriate places to learn such things.

I did not know these truths that night. I only knew that despite being alone in the house, I was not afraid, and despite my yearning for the company of the family, when Auntie Jean called my name on their arrival home, I did not answer, even though she came right to the door of the room where I lay, and called several times. The next day she told me she had brought me home an ice cream cone. I was sorry to have missed it, but said nothing, left the house and went down to the seashore, where I was not supposed to go alone. I sat on a high rock and watched the sea hit the round beach stones, felt and heard and saw the long coming in and going out of the sea. If you do that for long enough the sea eventually rhythms your blood's ebb and flow. On that day I no longer heard or saw or thought the sea; I was the sea and it was me. When I returned to my grandmother's house they were all in a fright; I had been away for hours it seems. It had felt like minutes. That was the day I learned the magic of disappearing into the rhythm of surf, how you could lose yourself so that time stopped, no tangled theology could bother your head, no language abused you or was abused by you, no grandmothers could bruise your heart. For there you had no heart or head, no consciousness. But the real magic was how you felt afterwards. It does not last very long, but for a short while you feel immune to the invasion of the world. Coming home to the worried household, I felt none of the emotions little girls are supposed to feel when they have frightened others with their absence. I did not feel sorry, I did not feel defensive, I did not feel apologetic. I was not part of them, I was not myself, I was away. I have gone to that away place often since, using the sound of water on shore to get there, the high fast waves of my vast prairie lake, or the longer rolls of this southern ocean.

Today, as I write, I realize I have found a way to multiply the effect of the surf on my arteries and veins. I have been writing this memoir of my girlhood with the window open, on a mild January day by the Gulf of Mexico. I have put words into the surf, and the push through my head is so sweet right now that I know I am finding a good place, a place where rhetoric meets the beat of the human heart, where place and self and art are matched. I am heading up the South Side Hill with such vigour that no trees can stop me, I carry the sea with me, spilling not a drop as I travel. I am learning to know my place; it is just ahead of me.

School: Losing Mary Lou; Finding Sally

*E*ven writing the word "school" is an accomplishment for me, one fairly recently gained. For most of my life I could never quite spell the word. Did it have two *l's* instead of two *o's*? Was it not *shc* instead of *sch*? All possibilities looked completely reasonable to me, and still do. But I now know how to spell the word because I've been to so many schools, taught in so many, that I have finally memorized the spelling of the word. SCHOOL. The order of the letters still looks so odd to me that I just used my "spell-check" to assure myself. It tells me I spelled it correctly. School is not the only word I have trouble with. I have trouble with mountains of words. All words with *sion* and *tion*, with double *c* and double *s*, all that have *or, er* as well as *ie, ei, ant* and *ent*. I transplant *their* and *there* and *too* and *to* even though I know the rules of their use well. The rules have been clanging in my head from grade one onward. I have good spelling days and bad spelling days, days when I know there is an "e" in foreground and days when I do not. Days when *necessary* slips out onto my computer screen with aplomb and days when it insists on being *neccesary*, and I cannot see its error to correct it.

Since the invention of the computerized spell-check, I can at least fool some of my colleagues into thinking that I am one of them. Before computers I would get my husband to check all my academic papers. He knew how necessary this was since I had once written a letter to an aunt, spelling that word as "anut" throughout. Richard pointed out the error and suggested I should rewrite the letter. At first I countered with the idea that maybe she, like I, would not notice. He gave me a look which made me understand that only I could believe spelling was unimportant. He has been proved correct in his concerns about my spelling.

103

When I wrote my entrance exams for Ph.D. studies in English the jury's comment was that the "candidate has a definite problem with spelling." My grade one teacher at Holloway School in St. John's, Newfoundland, said the same thing and assigned my mother to go over words that I was having trouble with. I remember working with Mom for what seemed like hours on getting the difference between the spelling of "horse" and "house." I rehearsed them all the way to school before the spelling test, spelled them correctly on the test, and then continued to confuse them for years whenever they appeared close to each other in any written passage. In my own little personal essays, houses regularly grazed in waving fields of hay and horses offered refuge and warmth to the weary traveller. The school system tried every method on me, from phonics to memorization, and still I spell terribly, despite the fact that I have read a good-sized library full of well-spelled books.

I confound my problem by unlearning spelling. Last year a young doctoral student asked me to explain to her the theory behind my use of the term "ungoing" which I had used several times in an unpublished essay of mine I had given her to read. It was a draft copy not yet spell-checked. I had to admit that this was not a new term I had invented, but was in fact the word "ongoing," a word I've only recently learned to mis-spell. I mumbled some joke about academic dyslexia and she tried not to look shocked.

Despite my spelling, and my grammar (yes, I make continuing errors in verb agreement, I misplace my modifiers, misuse possessives), I have always felt myself to be smarter than the people around me. In fact, it is not until the last few years that I have actually discovered that there are a few people who are as smart as or smarter than me, and since most of them are crazy, they don't matter. This conviction may surprise anybody who knows me in my professional life where I suspect I have a reputation as a naïve, rather verbose, well-meaning, but essentially unsophisticated literary critic, who, while opinionated, practises the usual female-forelock pulling of making light of her own ideas. Despite my learned femininity, my conviction of my own brilliance came early in life and has not left me. However, attendance at school offered the most serious of challenges to it, and I had to learn a trick or two to hold on to my belief in myself.

Richard has just read this passage and finds five errors. I will spell-check them before you read this. He says that I also use hyphens and ellipses incorrectly and theorizes that I make these mistakes because I consider these things too trivial to learn. I don't think he is entirely right, since I make these errors not because I think they don't matter, but because I am convinced I am right. I do check words I am unsure of (like *ellipses*) and whenever I do, I find the spell-check in agreement with me. It's the ones I am certain of that are incorrect. At any rate, Richard thinks I don't notice detail because details are trivial to me. And I agree in part: the details of factual observation that are important to him, the colour of a gull's eye, the difference between poison ivy and sarsaparilla, details of the physical universe that we receive through our eyes, rather bore me. Since I could hardly see the blackboard at school until I got corrective lenses at age ten, I was not as visually dependent as was normal, so I probably still take other senses more seriously than sight. The only time I took sight seriously was when I was colouring. Four inches from a page, with the smell of waterpaints circling pleasantly in my head, I loved the sight of my own choices in colours, whether they be an accurate reflection of the physical world around me or not. But therein lay part of my problem. I did not give enough credence to the line that is drawn between reality and fantasy; I was always aware of its shifting nature, therefore I was not too concerned with being as exact as is proper about what is called fact. And I suppose that problem began with having a pretend friend who became real.

Mary Lou arrived in my life very early, because I do not remember being without her. My mother testifies that my imaginary Mary Lou was so real to me that once, while we rushed to get a streetcar at the convergence of Topsail Road and Waterford Bridge Road, I suddenly stopped dead in my tracks screaming in panic, and despite all Kathleen's efforts to make me move, I resisted, claiming that Mary Lou had not kept up with us and would be lost and alone if we got on the car without her. Mother decided that since I was now well into my fifth year of existence it was about time I lived in the real world. She picked me up and rushed for the now-moving streetcar. I proceeded to become hysterical, unholdable, throwing a tantrum more suited to one half my age and attracting attention from people on the street. Needless to say, we missed the streetcar. Kathleen and I stood side by side at the car stop, she angry and frightened, me sobbing with great stuttering sobs as I waited for poor Mary Lou to catch up to me.

Last night I watched one of those television shows that investigates real domestic life as if it were newsworthy, using interview and voice-over techniques that give it the feel of both factual and autobiographical reality. I love this kind of television. I've heard it called "trash TV," and like all forms which use autobiographical reference it is kind of trashy, dependent on a combination of all sorts of suspect information and personal impressions taken from the trash can of more respected discourses, usually brought to bear on something not considered very important in the world of mainstream public knowledge. The problem last night was corporal punishment and alternatives to hitting your kids in order to discipline them. One video byte showed two-year-olds having tantrums and demonstrated typical parental choices of picking up the child to comfort it or smacking it to put it right again. Both were wrong according to the child expert. He showed experiments where parents placed the child in a "time out" place near the parent, but not obtrusively so. Then the parent would play games or enter into interesting activities that the child would probably like to join in, but could not until the crying finished. It worked. The expert said the parents would be giving the child an invaluable skill, the ability of self-control.

Somehow I never got self-control. I think you need self-control to be a responsible adult and notice the colour of the gull's eye and spell correctly. It's hard to decide how I missed this emotional equipment. My parents' theory seems to be that it is something you are born with and I didn't have it from the beginning. Let me nuance that. Getting me to a non-hysterical state in my early childhood seemed to them to be a matter of luck more than good management. In my cranky babyhood, screaming was relieved by the motion of trains and cars. Later, being taken on expeditions with my father to give my mother some relief—to his office for instance—seemed to calm me down. My dad tells me I first held a pencil to paper on one of our expeditions. At nine months I used to like to sit at my father's desk and pretend I was writing. Maybe that's how I became a daddy's girl. When he went to war, mother had to allow me to stand at the window keening "my daddy gone, neber took me," because despite the fact that it drove her crazy, it had, ironically, a calming effect on me, the repetition becoming a kind of moan of chronic pain rather than the hysteria that ensued as soon as my mother tried to take me from the window to comfort me in her arms. Later, my mother had the good luck to discover Mary Lou. When I would do some bad thing like dragging a teddy bear across the wet soapy floor my mother was scrubbing, or knocking over all the cups and glasses within my reach, my mother would try to explain to me that my behaviour was inappropriate. I think she must have tried to be fairly calm about this, since I already had a reputation for wild reactions. But I gather it rarely worked. Any attempt to assign responsibility and teach me new behaviours were short-circuited by my quite instant and compelling tantrums. To calm me my mother took to holding me in front of the mirror, distracting me by pointing to my reflection and asking me who the little girl was in the mirror and then asking me what I would do if my face froze in that contorted position. I preferred the first question to the second, even then being one who thought more about issues of identity than issues of cause and effect.

Who actually decided to answer "Mary Lou" to the question of the identity of the little girl in the mirror is still at issue between my mother and me, but naming seemed to offer a solution for both of us. Apparently I quickly learned to go on at great lengths about all the bad things Mary Lou did. Mother thought it was my way of owning up to my little crimes. Poor Mother. This was one more incident in my history of overturning her every effort to get me to grow up. Soon I was taking Mary Lou everywhere, loving her company despite the fact that she engaged in dreadful behaviours.

Since I want to avoid telling you lies, I have begun to consult with my parents—who have arrived here in Florida for some vacation time—about these little anecdotes I am telling you. Last night I drove them up the coast to their favourite Greek restaurant and subtly pumped them about my fifth year of life. I wanted to get past my mother's usual stories about Mary Lou and the streetcar, Mary Lou and me and the mirror. But my parents have started to change their attitudes concerning my childhood. I think they have got the idea from the things I've asked and the fact that I spend the mornings hiding away with my word processor, that I am writing these bits about my childhood and suddenly they seem to have agreed on a party line. I was, according to my mother's new version, a sensible child, no hysteria, no developmental problems, no trouble! "You were sensitive, and just . . . well, imaginative." My father nods in agreement. When I ask where Mary Lou came from, Mother shrugs and says I just told her one day that I had "a little friend." No big deal, no theories of delayed development and the division of the self. My parents will have none of my belief that the female child can be rendered powerless in language because the parts of her self unallowed by patriarchy make constant war against her. I don't even try to mention such hypotheses.

"Lots of children have imaginary friends," says my dad, the child expert. "It's quite common you know."

So where is the difficult and hysterical child I have been hearing about for over four decades now? Once upon a time when I confessed to my mother that I was seeing a psychiatrist, she asked my dad if he could guess which one of his five children would be most likely to need such help. She told me that he answered "Helen" without a moment's pause. So they must have known the child that became so dear to me over a decade of therapy. Eating our Greek salad as the sun sets over the shrimp boats of Tarpon Springs, I feel a rage coming on. In a moment I may start throwing a tantrum right here between the tables of the crowded restaurant, dragging my feet as my embarrassed parents try to haul me to the car, screaming at them to give me back the dyslexic, hysterical child they have robbed from me.

"You weren't dyslexic, what a word—*dyslexic*! You just started school a year early because I lied about your age." I calmly eat another slice of bread spread amply with the butter I do not allow myself at home and imagine myself throwing a tantrum in the restaurant aisle, under the feet of the busy waitresses, as my mother explains that Holloway School, the best United Church school in St. John's, would take children who turned five by February of the school year, but since I would not be five until March 28, 1946, I was ineligible. Mother needed me to be in school. Being an "imaginative" child I probably required a lot of attention, probably got bored easily, probably begged to go to school like my big brother.

Speaking of that worthy fellow, I know my parents are revising my life because after telling about lying to get me into school Mom asks if I remember how the neighbour boy who was supposed to help me transfer from one streetcar to another on the way to school lost me one day. He ran to catch the second one and left me behind. Now I have a very good memory of that event, of standing alone on a corner of Water Street and weeping until a policeman came along, elicited my parents' last name, phoned my mother who told him to put me on the streetcar home where she met me in none too sympathetic a mood. I remember all too clearly who the male culprit was: it was my older brother, no neighbour boy; it was my very own older brother, who would prefer to risk losing a sister rather than risk being late for school. I don't blame him. I know what he would have gotten if he were late—three sharp hits from the leather strap that Miss Leslie, the principal, kept in her office. He made a wise decision. I don't fault him. I, too, have felt the edge of Miss Leslie's strap and understand fully. It's my parents I'm angry at. How dare she try to change the cast of characters after all these years? It's a blatant effort at revisionary history, and I will have none of it.

I do not throw the tantrum in the restaurant, although it has been delicious imagining it. Like sitting in church and imagining yourself suddenly rising and spitting out pornographic plots. I realize now that I'm sort of on my own with these stories. Those smooth-tongued, sly elders, Harold and Kathleen, my mommy and daddy of yesteryear, have become unreliable narrators.

It's not as if I want to portray myself as a precocious child capable of overthrowing parental rule with my craziness. I just wanted my own way a lot. I was willful. Lots of kids are willful. Like my oldest son who undertook to undermine our decision to teach him not to touch his father's books when he was one year old. Being silly young parents we thought we would teach him territorial imperatives. The plan was to make the house childproof except for one item, a small bookcase of books. This would limit the things to which we had to say no. Then we would insist on this one no-no until he learned to play with his own toys and leave the books alone. Then, the plan went, we would add other forbidden items one by one, until our house once more had our possessions within the easy and carelessly cluttered reach that Richard preferred. Our son ended the no campaign simply by turning it on us. Whenever he pulled out a few books, dangling them precariously by their covers, we would put them back, all the while saying "No, NO, the books are a NO-NO." Looking at us with furrowed brow he would immediately pull some more books out, all the while saying "no, no, no, no." Pretty soon he was following us around answering any attempt at conversation with that single word NO. In the middle of the night we would hear him practising in his crib. NO, NO, NO, NO, NO, NO, NO, NO, NO. We gave up as we later would with our daughter, who liked to colour on walls. We tried giving her really large pieces of paper, the kind used by artists and architects on big drafting boards, showing her that this gave her as much scope as walls did. She was a quiet, obedient child and accepted the papers willingly, getting to work immediately to cover every inch with her strange swirling patterns. She also took to waking up at six o'clock in the morning, while her parents were still snoring, to cover the real walls with her artistic endeavours. When we were old enough that we should have known better our youngest son rewarded our little pep talks about living a more energetic, less passive teenagehood, our ploys of removing television and other entertainments from his life, by sleeping for incredibly long periods of time—would you believe twenty hours—after each lecturette or new house rule.

I tell you this to indicate that I am not Napoleonic enough in this ego trip of self-writing to believe I was actually doing anything unique in my subversive elaboration of Mary Lou. Watching that television show about how to train your kids out of their tantrums I had the distinct feeling that experts and parents alike were underestimating the cleverness of all kids. What really interests me here, concerning devices that parents and children invent collaboratively to induce civilized behaviour, is what happens when you have to lose the invented device before you are ready to let it go. We've all heard of kids who had trouble going to school without their frayed security blankets. I think Mary Lou was in that category. My mother admits now that I was sent to school too early. You see, I think I had my mother convinced of my brilliance too. Most of the time she had on her hands this curious, inventive, imperiously confident, verbally proficient child (except when she tried to correct my behaviour in which case I became unmanageable). School would give my brain and my imagination something worthwhile to do, and it would surely teach me the one thing she had not been able to teach me, self-control. Rational thinking like this has led many a mother down the garden path.

I knew the moment I was sitting behind one of those serious square desks, looking around at all the other serious square desks in a formation of a rectangle so that we little students all faced each other, that this was no place for Mary Lou; she would not survive this place. I had to ditch her. I had to forget her. I had to go on without her. Without Mary Lou I had to sit silently watching all those other girls who looked so confident. They had probably turned five, I thought. My mother had told me not to tell my birthday, so I knew that I was there as an impostor. If I'd had Mary Lou, I could have impressed these kids with my friend's capacity for jokes and tricks, but I instinctively knew that Mary Lou and I would get into dreadful trouble if we showed off here. As it was, I had nothing to say, and nobody had anything to say to me. Our teacher, Miss Dingle (yes, she was actually called that and turned out to be as sweet and pleasant as her name), explained how you must put up your hand to go to the bathroom, and then took us on a tour of that facility. As soon as we went back to the classroom I put up my hand to go, and she let me, after explaining that each child had the right to go only once in the morning (of course we could go all we wanted at recess), so this would be my occasion. I realized I was using up my privilege, but I had a desperate feeling of being without Mary Lou and I needed to find her. Perhaps I had left her in the washroom. When I got there it was not the jolly place it had been with all the other children, but a cool, lonely, hollow space, all red-tiled and filled with a subdued light and silence. Trying to get into the swing of things, be a good schoolgirl, I gamely pulled down my underpants and sat down to pee. Suddenly, terror rushed in from every corner of the room and I pulled up my pants and rushed away. I do not know if I left Mary Lou in the first floor girls' washroom at Holloway School in St. John's, Newfoundland, in September of 1945; I just know that she was not with me after that and I may have given up the part of me that might be able to learn to spell properly. I gave up talking to the mirror, although, as an adult, I sometimes talk to myself while driving, and occasionally now, as I age, I find myself talking back to the idiots on the evening news.

At school, without Mary Lou, in the place I was supposed to learn self-control, I learned something quite different. I learned that life was a continuing effort in trying to please the people in control, people who keep wanting you to do things that your own brilliance finds incredibly wrong-headed. So I tried to please them, still do, while the voice in my head undermines my best efforts at pleasing. I have always failed, but with failure came the real learning: I learned to cover my growing impostorhood with artifice. And I am still learning.

At first school was kind of fun, but then it was just kindergarten and I suppose we were being socialized for our future careers as students. Little did I know that all that wonderful sweeping and swirling over acres of paper with my water colours was training the small muscles I would need for printing and writing. I, an overly serious little innocent with my jam-jar of water, brought ever so carefully from the tap to my desk, with my twelve little pellets of colour (including black and white), knew nothing of the hidden agendas of my teacher. I worked carefully to use just the right amount of moisture to get the pad of colour working for me, then took off. Blue I loved. My skies were so big you would think I already lived on the Prairies. There were days that black was so intensely powerful that all the people in my pictures were black.

"But Helen, all your people are black," said Miss Dingle. "Yes," said I, "and I haven't finished. There will be black cats too!" "Hmm," observed Miss Dingle, leaving me alone to pursue my vision of suppressed power.

I remember when my daughter's nursery-school teacher came to our house one day, displayed a water colour which was a great sweeping mess of purple and black and told us that when asked what the story of her picture was, the child had, sobbing throughout, told of being lost in the woods and her father coming to rescue her. "The little thing was so upset, I nearly cried myself," observed the well-meaning woman. "Yes?" queried I. "Well, don't you think this darkness, and the crying—you should have heard her sobs—is something to be worried about?" "Hmm," said I, wishing Miss Dingle had let me tell her the story of my blackness.

I have always been fascinated by my daughter's ability, now disciplined by years of theatre training, to contain and use emotion productively. Without Mary Lou, I had no proper outlet for all that seething emotion. But soon, the disciplines of schooling arrived to drive me into reason.

Back there in kindergarten I should have known when we were given little pictures to colour with crayons, that something untoward was happening. But the controllability of crayons compared to soggy paint brushes, the glory of two shades of "flesh" colour (one pinky, one pinky-brown), and the delightful little pictures of elves with pointy ears, boys with sweet little cowlicks that you could colour red, and girls with full swinging dresses with hems that swept around their thighs, dresses which you could colour red and green and blue and orange (never yellow; I hated yellow) kept me from realizing the real intent of this move from free-flow soggy water colours to crayons and gestetnered outlines: we were to learn to colour inside the lines. It is only now—looking over some of the curriculum materials from the forties that I carefully photocopied when I realized I couldn't remember what I had studied in school—that I realize the true insidiousness of this move: once we learned to colour inside the lines we were only one step away from what the adults really wanted us to do: arithmetic.

In the beginning arithmetic was all right, not fun, but full of prestige. By now I was in grade one, and there had to be something to allow you a proper measure of scorn for the little kids in kindergarten. Arithmetic was just the thing. Walking to the streetcar after school with my

Caribou Arithmetic Number Stories in my book bag, with the knowledge that I had "homework", unlike the little kids who had no such important responsibilities, made up for the fact that arithmetic was the silliest thing the school system had asked me to do so far. Even the cover of Caribou Arithmetic was silly. Yes, there were two sensible-looking caribou, profiled just like the bronze caribou in Bowring Park that I liked to go to see whenever we went there to swim in the summer. But they were in the top corners of the cover and were so minuscule they hardly made up for the rest of the display. For a start, a boy and girl were holding hands. Imagine that! In our school, boys were in classrooms on the other side of the building, in the section we only went to when sent with a note from our teacher to one of their teachers, or—terror of terrors—when we were sent to see Miss Leslie, the principal. Holding hands with a boy was beyond the pale. But even excusing this gaff on the part of the Caribou Arithmetic people, what do you think the boy and girl were doing with their free hands? They were greeting the oddest creatures I'd ever seen, creatures with elfin heads, not cute ones like in our kindergarten colouring exercises, but malicious-looking creatures with large-featured faces, enormous pointed ears, grins as phony as your brother's when he is about to snitch on you. I have since learned that these creatures are more properly called gnomes, a rather grotesque version of elf, but to this day I don't know why the Caribou Arithmetic people would choose them for their cover. It was not user-friendly. Even in my sixth decade of life I still have nights when, in that moment of selflessness between awake and sleep, their grotesque faces etch and dissolve beneath my eyelids.

The faces weren't the worst of it. They also had froglike legs with knobby knees and gigantic pointed feet. But the very, very most terrible feature of all was their bodies. Their bodies were numbers! The zero didn't look too bad, just rotund, but the four looked like he had an angular growth out of his belly, seven seemed to have an extra arm, and six looked like he was leaning backwards at at an incredible angle in order to support the outrageous loop of the six which was his belly. Thank goodness none of the bodies were female! Most disgusting of all was number one who had his back to the viewer. Because the pica points at the bottom of the number continued on to meet his frog-like legs, he was bent for all the world as if he'd been caught shitting on the page. Unfortunately, I could not verify this as the part that would be his backside was hidden behind the words "GINN AND COMPANY:

TORONTO" in very large print. But he did look as if he were about to plant a big crapola right where it said "material contained in this book is fully protected by copyright." Of course I couldn't read those words then, but I could certainly read the angle of that gnome's body.

As far as I was concerned, arithmetic continued to be silly, even scatological. The Caribou people, with my teachers' keen complicity, required me to colour the second of a set of four ducks which had wheels instead of feet, or colour the third of a row of objects that they refused to identify. They looked a bit like spinning tops, but by the time I decided they were really Christmas decorations and needed a red and green treatment, teacher was ready for us to move on to the next exercise. Being the kind of girl who liked to finish a job, I particularly resented leaving six of seven sailboats or houses uncoloured. Sometimes there were minutes at the end of the day when we were allowed to go back and colour in the extra cakes or cups or cats, but since I was slow at arithmetic I generally had to use my time to complete the exercises. What a relief it was in summer holidays, when we could take our old Caribou workbooks home, to colour in the whole row of mittens or pussycats or balloons. I used to play school with younger children and make them colour whole rows of dolls and balls and dogs and boys and sheep and piglets and birds and flowers and kites and boats and girls with curly hair and girls with pigtails. I probably disadvantaged the little ones of my neighbourhood forever as they headed off to real school a year or two later convinced that arithmetic was about colouring lovely rows of ducks.

As with their covers the Caribou people often had an inappropriate sense of decorum in their arithmetic problems. In one exercise called "fun with hearts" we were to colour four hearts red and three hearts blue. Blue! Can you believe it? The possibility staggered me. I may have taken poetic licence with mitts or hens or oranges, but I was pretty strict on the subject of hearts and valentines. If, when counting up the number of valentines you received from the classroom valentine box as teacher read out the recipient of each one—so that numbers really were important—if when your heart was beating faster to see if Marilyn or Margery had failed to remember you after you had hinted that they were on your list, what if someone had given you a blue valentine? Well, who would be the bigger fool, you or her? However, something told me that the case was more serious than this, that indeed these blue hearts had something to do with the "blue babies" I had heard mothers talking about. Did blue babies have blue hearts? I felt that the Caribou people had gone further than silly; their questions, like their covers, had violated good taste in bringing up such a subject.

In fact, they were worse than that; they withheld what I considered pertinent information. Take, for example, an exercise which showed fifteen little men with elfin hats, but baby faces (the usual pointed ears), who were setting off in two boats stupidly named A and B. (Couldn't they think up better names than that? All you had to do was walk down to the harbour to find all the names you might need, from Little Marianne to Bay Bulls Bully.) The exercise wanted me to colour six caps yellow and nine caps red then add and subtract these, while figuring out how many little men were in each boat by covering one and counting the figures in the other, all of this with not even a scrap of information about where they were going on their boat ride, even though one of them was enthusiastically pointing off to the left margin of the page. But this narrative incompleteness was surpassed by the fact that the exercise was entitled "The Brownies Go for a Boat Ride." Brownies? Brownies! This was too much. I protested to teacher: "How can these little men be Brownies? Everyone knows that Brownies are for girls age seven to ten." (I knew this because I had to wait a half-year later than everyone else in my class to join the companionship of the toadstool, my true age having been revealed midway through grade one.) Teacher must have been used to such questions, for the tone of her voice had that edge which said "this had better be the very last time you ask me something today": "Call them elves or whatever you want, Helen. There will still be fifteen of them to add and subtract no matter what you call them." Silenced, but outraged at this violation of naming, I put my face the usual four inches from my book and taking a comforting sniff of my red crayon set unwillingly to work.

By the time I graduated to book two of the Caribou arithmetic series (same indecent cover) things had gone from frustrating to alarming. Pictures had exited, and now I was faced with page after page of numbers informed only by words. Not being able to count the number of little flower buds or toy horns in one pictorial group and then subtract the lesser number in the other group, I was forced into subterfuge. We were not supposed to use our fingers to help us with our adding and subtracting, but if you hid your fingers under your desk you could sometimes escape teacher's attention. Failing that, you could wiggle your toes and envision them separately to help you with addition and subtraction. However, once into 6 + 2 + 4 you needed fingers and toes together. It got pretty risky when teacher patrolled our straight rows of desks.

Up and down, up and down she went, as I waited for that brief interval after she had passed my desk and before she turned again at the end of the row. It sometimes felt as if all my real learning took place in those milliseconds when I was not under surveillance. In that moment I would rush to add up fingers, pencils, erasers, even the pigtails of the girl ahead of me in my effort to find out the answer to anything over ten. Long gone now was the companionable rectangle of kindergarten. From now on interaction between students would be banned, all dealings being private ones between each student and the teacher, all knowledge acquisition a capitalistic enterprise marked by my inability to accomplish the tasks in good enough time to get the treasured commodity of the gold star. I had to be satisfied with red and blue stars, the consolation prizes of our competitive exchange system.

Insidiously emphasizing this competitive system were the bold letters appearing at the bottom of each exercise: "Of these 33 (or 25, or 19) examples, I tried _____ ; I had _____ right." This kind of self assessment made me nervous, disturbed my sense of my own brilliance. I had never tried or correctly completed enough in the time allotted and the difference between "I tried" and "I had right" was often abysmal. Mother, who had valiantly attempted to teach me the difference between "horse" and "house," was once more called into service, to little effect. In fact, when, more than a decade later, I had sweated my way to trigonometry, my father thought he would inform me about the practical uses of tangents and cosigns, a down-to-earth application of knowledge my mathematics teachers had failed to give me. With this new knowledge he believed my love of the subject would catch fire. He drew bridges and other complex structures all over my workbook. To no avail. He was fighting a lifetime of my weird adjustment to mathematics, an adjustment that allowed me to just barely accomplish what the school system required without ever understanding what they wanted me to learn. He finished in frustration, saying "I just can't figure out how your mind works." Subversively, I would have told him if I'd known the word then.

It got so that the only time I liked arithmetic even a little bit was when we practiced "tables" aloud. Always a good faker, then and now, and with everyone in the class repeating the answers, I could mouth along, safe in the anonymity of the group. As years went by, a new linguistic (as opposed to pictorial) approach to arithmetic was particularly disquieting because so many interesting stories were only half told. Take the one that went, "Kate spent 7 cents for an orange and 8 cents on some figs. How much did she spend for both?" I knew the answer, but between reading the sentence and recording fifteen, there was a long intake of breath when I wondered about "some figs." The only figs I knew came squashed into square slabs in packages that my mother bought for baking. Little girls certainly could not go to a store and buy "some figs." I would then have to make an effort to drive this speculation out of my mind in order to record the answer. By then many of my classmates had already answered the next question, "Ida read 8 pages in her new storybook yesterday, and 6 today. How many pages did she read in all?" While the top achievers rushed on to how many blocks Margaret lived from school and the problem of Joe's egg purchases, I was still asking how long might it take for Margaret to read 8 pages, imagining what kind of storybook she had and hoping it was a nice long one with good pictures.

At the end of the year, when the "prize list" of the top twelve students was announced, I was amazed to learn I was not on it. How could a person feel so smart and not be among the top twelve? Having spent a year wondering about the possible titles and contents of Alice's three green books, four red books, three blue books and two brown books, and imagining how wonderful it was to actually own twelve books, I felt completely devastated to learn I was not inside the discipleship of those that were named by teacher. I fleetingly thought of leaving my school career behind and going on to something more profitable; however, there was the ever-to-be-desired new readers that would come up in the next year. The expectation of new readers was worth putting up with all the arithmetic they could throw at me, even if, as was threatened, something called multiplication and long division were to be part of my future.

And speaking of school readers, I've been alive in this female body for more than half a century now and I can truly say that I have learned at least one lesson right down to my bone marrow: the patriarchy chains you on the very grounds of your own desire. Yes, dear reader, it's that time again: feminist message moment. We pause in our hunger for narrative to let me take you by your shoulders and tell you to listen up. Breathe deeply. Get ready for your medicine. To be fair, I offer you the opting-out formula: don't read any further, skip some pages until you're sure I'm finished with my "message," or do as I do when I don't like the direction a plot is taking: write your own story.

And for you feminists out there, aging and minoritized, who are a little impatient with me for this interruption, this special pleading, remember where we are—not in our hearts and heads—but in time and history. We have begun to have an effect on ideology—not that anyone wants to admit it—but our small successes have caused the inevitable backlash. I have to take that backlash into consideration. Even five years ago when I would tell my classes I was a feminist—in the name of getting ideology up front—I got a mixture of suspicion, hostility and grudging respect. Promising emotions to work with for a teacher. Now I get indulgent smiles, the sort of "lighten up, Granny" attitude that is so much more effective at defeating you than taking you seriously would be. I have to ride those smiles, use them for my own purposes, be ever so humorous too, because if I do anything else I'm dead in the water: old and old-fashioned and not nice. Being not nice is a serious offence for older women. So we must play to their smiles, waiting for the right moment to turn a corner as they laugh at our little satires. But as we seem to exit, leaving them laughing, we are not leaving them at all; we are going right inside their heads. Don't worry that I have given anything away; they're not reading this part. So let's see how I do. Stay with me, daughters of Virginia, I may need your help.

I loved reading. There are no qualifiers to that sentence; I simply loved to read. Before I could read I used to watch my dad read the newspaper before dinner while Mom was cooking in the kitchen and wonder what mental operation was needed to do that work. Of course, I appreciated the fact that reading newspapers was incompatible with making meals and cleaning up after them. I liked that too. I have been so grateful to the school system for teaching me how to read that I have stayed with the education business in one way or another ever since. Each year of my childhood—returning to the classroom to face more defeats in arithmetic and spelling—I was comforted by the thought that there would be new readers. At the end of the first day of school each year we would go home to cover our books with the school-issued brown-paper covers which would protect them so that they could be used next year by another class. I loved covering my books; I liked cutting carefully down the dotted lines at the top and bottom of the middle of the brown-paper so you could create the little strip that would be folded inside the spine of the book, a task requiring great nimbleness. I liked making the tight square corners that left no give in the paper so that the cover would last all year with one dab of glue in each corner holding brown paper to brown paper. I liked to look at the cover of the readers a long time before I covered them, for I would not see them again for ten whole months when the brown paper covers—by then marked with every kind of doodle known to children—would come off again and reveal the slick newness of their happy faces.

Happy they were. On the cover of *Fun with Dick and Jane*, there was the friendliest brother and sister I'd ever seen, talking to each other about Dick's new toy airplane. And down in the corner, below the title, was Spot, the cutest dog in the whole world, looking up at these two delightful children. On the cover of *Friends and Neighbours*, a little girl with really nice pigtails (thick like mine never were) and her little male friends are being approached by a clown with two enormous bundles of balloons which stand way up in the air in multicoloured splendour. My hands touch the cover; I am sure he is holding his right hand out towards the girl; her hand points: any moment now she will open all her fingers, rotate her hand to bring the palm outward. She will fold her fingers carefully around the strings of the balloons, so that not one will fly away and they will laugh together, the clown and the girl. Then the boy will be given his balloons and the girl will use her free hand to pull the wagon that sits beside her on the cover (I'm quite sure it's hers), and off they will go to a whole reader full of adventures. I loved making stories of the covers, and indeed it was a good thing I did, because the stories inside were not quite as I would have had them in my imagination.

Inside *Friends and Neighbours* for example, the very first story tells of how Jill and Ann hear some boys calling them to "Come and Play with Us." The girls look all around and can find no one: "There was no one in the yards. There was no one on the walks, and no one on all of Pleasant Street." The little girls were not, as you might suspect, the survivors of a nuclear holocaust, but rather the butts of a rather nasty male joke. It seems the boys have stolen the girls' dolls. The girls find various notes that direct them where to go in no uncertain terms and when they finally arrive at the apple tree, they find the smiling little boys with the dolls alive and unharmed. This little kidnapping scenario may well have rubbed me the wrong way in grade two, since I had already had the experience of facing down some neighbourhood boys who were trying to murder my older brother. He had judged that discretion was the better part of valour and fled, but I, appalled at this blow to the family honour, had faced them in the street and taunted them with, "You want to hit Clarkes? I'm a Clarke, come try and hit me. Just try and hit ME!" I repeated over and over. They paced the road a measured distance from me, until David had time to tell Mom what was happening and she called me in. Not satisfied with my victory I had called them "sissies" over my shoulder as I ambled toward home. David assured me he would pay for my behaviour and that the only reason I had not been slaughtered was that I was a girl. I had felt it was my commanding voice and presence, but that is beside the point. The point is that even then I was suspicious of unsupervised little boys, and I was disturbed by this doll-snatching story and not very pleased when the girls agreed to accept rides on the boys' wagons.

The girls in the picture are waving like little milksops as the boys approach, pushing their wagons with one foot inside, one on the sidewalk. And there they are again, those wimpy little girls, holding on for dear life as the boys steer the wagon handles and bend over to push faster and faster. I knew of no boy in my neighbourhood who would ever offer to push me, or even nicer girls in their wagons. And even if they did I could tell that a girl in such a situation had no control over the speed of the wagon, and you wouldn't catch me on the road with a speed maniac. Having your own wagon was the only solution and indeed that was what I asked for and got that very Christmas. It only partially assuaged my disappointment that the wagon on the cover of my reader, now covered by brown paper, did not belong to the girl.

Of course what bothers me now is quite different: it's those damn notes the boys wrote, leading the girls on to the desired object, their dolls. I don't care that the notes frame themselves in affection and fun: "Dear Jill and Ann, look for the dolls in the. . . ." Following these words appears a drawing of two dolls in a swing (an obvious clue) and then a drawing of three little stick men with hats and printed below the little men are the names of Billy, Tom and Joe. Staring at this illustration of little boy/men in my old school reader, from the hideous awareness of half a century of female life, I want to scream at the top of my lungs, warning Jill and Ann: "They are roping you in with desire for your dolls, desire goaded on by the language of their writing. They will own you as surely as they own those little stick men in hats." But no use. Jill and Ann were not listening then; they are not listening now. Chained to men's language by their desire for their dolls, they rush with glee, ransom note in hand, around the neighbourhood to various hiding places until finally they gratefully accept the gift of their hijacked dolls from the boys who have led them along with words as if it were the most natural thing in the world for males to set the conditions of the possession of our dolls, our babies. But as I said, I loved reading, so something had to happen to allow me to go on reading happily in the readers the ideology of my time provided for me.

Writing the last line of the previous paragraph brought me to the end of a rush of memory-making. I felt empty; I also felt like a fraud, because I'm constructing this version of myself from the point of view of a woman in her fifties. I can't really give you the seven-year-old Helen who I now think must have swallowed these books like manna from heaven. She was so hungry to read that it all tasted good, and there in her hunger for language, her desire moving like quicksilver through the artery of narrative, she was caught. I've spent a day or two thinking about what I should say next. You see, despite the fact that I know that humour is my best bet, it's hard to maintain. This writing starts the anger again. I feel a bit like the philosopher Simone de Beauvoir who wrote (at about my time of life in her memoir of her mother) that when she looked back over her own brilliant career she felt robbed. Imagine that! With her privilege, her intelligence, her accomplishments she still felt something vital had been kept from her. I feel robbed too. Despite the safe privilege of my upbringing, I feel angry at the possibilities that were taken away from me by *Fun with Dick and Jane, Our New Friends, Friends and Neighbours,* and *More Friends and Neighbours.* These books did not open up the world for me; they were training manuals for gender roles.

Picture little me in grade three, opening the covers of *More Streets and Roads.* Little Molly Anne, who seems remarkably easy to hoodwink, is displayed looking first for a rooster, then a lion, under the furniture of her house, just because her Uncle George could throw his voice. Now my Uncle Charl could pull a nickel out of your ear, but that was different. We all knew it was a trick and tried to figure out how to do it. We couldn't, but that was OK since Uncle Charl gave you the nickel as reward for trying. The fact that a little girl would even contemplate the idea that a rooster, let alone a lion, was under the sofa was too much. How could anybody be expected to align herself with such an idiot. Later in the book Molly Ann is shown sacrificing part of her doll's silk skirt to patch the wing of Bob's toy airplane so he can win a contest.

Well and good, I would do the same for a friend, maybe even a brother in trouble. However, after Bob wins a new model airplane set, does he invite her to build it with him? No. He tells her he will call the new plane Lilly (after the doll). Big deal! There was obviously no benefit to helping a boy.

In *More Streets and Roads* Bob keeps getting to do all the fun things; he solves mysteries, builds things, has adventures, and dumb Patty and Molly Ann just sort of stand around. Even when they are cooking eggs for egg dyeing—involving kitchens, and stoves and other domestic settings—it's not only Bob's idea, but in the picture he is also dipping an egg into the pot, while Patty just stands there watching the water boil. The whole damn book is like this: Sam becomes a cowboy, Nick takes dangerous boat rides, Carlos (from South America) sells his produce, Sojo (in a turban) catches fish, and Herbert the squirrel learns to read. The message was not only international and interracial, but inter-species: girls have nothing to do with the world of action. The adventurous characters that filled my readers, Porky the porcupine, Cheeky the prairie dog, Streaky the opossum, Hopalong the rabbit and Skinny the young, grey fox were all referred to as "he." I could take a hint!

Certainly there are girls in these readers. There is Mary Ellen who "Finds a Way" to buy some pretty cloth for her grandmother. At first this story looks promising: "Mary Ellen and her grandmother live in a lonely cabin high up on a mountainside. Their home was far from any town." Wow! Wilderness women. They pile wood for the winter, they put away plenty of food: flour, pumpkins dried beans, apples, pota-toes, honey, jam and apple butter to name a few items. Soon, however, Step-Along the trader, a sort of one-man industrial revolution, arrives with his ribbons, pins and buttons, his nails, hammers, tacks and shiny, new pots and pans. It quickly becomes obvious that grandmother, this formerly hearty, independent woman, lusts after some blue cloth for a new dress. I could have accepted a lust for nails and hammers or a good saw, but the picture confirms her gendered choice. There she is grinning with unseemly desire for the cloth the man holds out. Of course there is no money for such luxuries. Our little Mary Ellen does not give up how-ever. Knowing how much her granny wants the cloth, she works out a plan for Step-Along to buy a night's lodging each time he comes by. Mary Ellen will prepare his bed and Granny will cook for him. In this way they will be able to buy the cloth on the installment plan. Quite the workable little barter system, but dependent on Mary Ellen drafting herself into the service industry at age seven. All I want to know is: can you tell me has this ever happened in real life, that little girls occupy their minds with the clothing needs of their grandmothers? The message was clear: I was a selfish little girl, since it would never occur to me to worry about the wardrobe of my mother, let alone my grandmother.

By the time I get to page 228 and another heroic maternal figure appears, I am justly suspicious. When will the clay feet enter? Mother and Betsy are alone, because Father and Ben have gone hunting (what else is new). Mother protects home and family by shooting a rather dreadful bear. I quote to make my point: "In a few minutes Mr. Chase and Ben came running out of the woods. As they ran, they called out questions. 'What is the matter? Why did you shoot?' "

"I shot a bear," answered Mother, still hugging the baby.

"Impossible!" cried Father. "How could you shoot a bear?"

"I aimed very carefully," Mother replied. "I think I hit him, but he went off into the forest. Father please take your gun and follow his trail."

I don't want to read the rest: how Dad kills the bear and he and Ben wink to each other in silent understanding about how it takes a man to do a man's job and then sweet little mother laughs too, because she knows it was her hubby that really finished off the bear: "How everyone laughed! Mother had seen Father's wink, also." And Betsy is not going to be allowed to forget her mother's failure and the less-than-supportive family reaction, for "after that every visitor was shown a big handsome bearskin on the hearth, which Father always called 'Mother's Bear.' "

Dear reader, I imagine you thinking, "It could not be all bad. Surely there was some part of some reader which was less oppressive than you have portrayed them?" Well, there was one. During my research for this memoir story at the Curriculum Materials Centre in the Faculty of Education of Newfoundland's Memorial University, while I browsed through the stacks of old texts not used in the schools for decades now, I found the delightful *Stories about Sally* by Eleanor Thomas. I was so excited I photocopied the whole damn book, and a pretty penny it cost me.

This is not baby Sally from the old Dick and Jane books, whose courage, curiosity and good cheer were safe enough virtues, since baby Sally was merely a pre-school toddler with lots of time to learn female compliance. This more grown-up Sally with the pleasant, carefree pageboy haircut, the gleeful, active smile and the hands always doing, doing, doing is my new feminist heroine; she is curious, adventurous, canny and humorous without sacrificing one ounce of human decency, generosity and just plain interrelational aptitude. She is also—and this may be the explanation of the above virtues—what we would call today, empowered. Open the book to page three and you will find a picture of Sally showing her toy boat to the teacher and other students, on page four she sails it and on pages five, six and seven she takes on administrative level tasks by arranging a visit to the classroom by her uncle, a prominent expert on all things of a marine nature. He, to his credit, is completely at Sally's disposal, never asking her silly questions like is there a lion under her bed. I can easily edit out the fact that when the uncle needs help setting up his audio-visual equipment it is a boy who plugs in the projector. After all, boys must be accommodated. In this book however, they appear pretty well equal to girls. Sally helps the new boy at school, Jack, meet the other children, but that's where Jack's plot ends. Sally's cousin Tim is often her companion, but their activities are gender-blended. The nicest thing about Tim is that he has a little vegetable garden and invites Sally to choose which veggies they will eat. She does, they harvest them together, wash them together and eat them together. I have no doubt they did the dishes together. Nice as Tim is, he doesn't have his kisser plastered over every page. Sally is the main character, and one thing I like about her is that she gets to go just about everywhere on the entire continent. Sally is no fixed pole; she is the roving star of my dreams. Watch Sally travel by plane, boat and car to deserts, mountains, lakes, lighthouses, cities, farms, dude ranches, orange groves and palm-shaded beaches! I am in heaven in Sally's book. What a wonderful author is Eleanor Thomas, Sally's creator.

In my adult life the actual process of travelling has always made me feel my own separateness, in a kind of freeing way. Before leaving I am someone's teacher, someone's wife, someone's mother, and after arriving I will be someone's guest lecturer, someone's audience, someone's examiner, but on the way, especially in the airports that are my usual places of transit, I am myself, unencumbered by roles, free to observe, to write, to read, or just watch the bartender. But Sally is not only the traveller in me, she is also the neighbourhood person that I have always wanted to be, but never have been since leaving the Avalon Peninsula in Newfoundland. As Sally tours around to fire stations, and bakeries, libraries and department stores, she is friends with everyone:

the devotees of Sunday schools, winter fairs, zoos and radio stations. She is on speaking terms with police and postal workers, store clerks and dairymen. I don't mind that she helps Aunt May with the grocery shopping, because she packs her bag right after and is off again on another adventure. Sally gets to make posters for the fair, own a duck, show Tim how the library works and helps make a new park possible. Sally is a person.

But in my secret heart of hearts what I like best about Sally is that she appears to be an only child. No siblings compete with her for parental attention. There is no elder brother for father to fret over, wondering if he will be able to take up his proper place in the patriarchy. There is no younger brother, fragile and accident-prone, to distract the maternal heart, no baby sister and brother to be used as training ground for Sally's maternality. When Sally goes on a summer vacation with her parents and stays at a cabin in a mountain park, it is Sally who helps her dad barbecue and put out the fire, it is Sally who learns to fish with Dad and ride a pony with the cowboys. It is Sally, Sally, Sally who comes home with her mom and dad to their pretty house and her cat Tar Baby, and makes a book of pictures about her summer vacation, with Mom and Dad smiling on, ready to help, but never interfering. Yes, dear reader, I confess. Like many children (especially female children) in multiple-child families, I have this guilty desire to be an only child.

Sally's story is the perfect antidote for my training as second-class citizen, except for one thing. The record of Newfoundland's curriculum tells me that although published in 1949, *Stories about Sally* did not get on the curriculum until 1951, by which time I was into grades five and six, well past the Ginn and Company readers series and into the discourses of nationalism and the literary tradition. Sally was not mine, not me, never could be me. My younger sister, Kathy, eight years younger than me, may well have met Sally. Perhaps that is what made her hitchhike all over a half-continent, undeterred by customs officials, serial killers and the worries of her older sister. "Just don't tell Mom," were her words as she flung her knapsack over her shoulders, strode out onto the Trans-Canada Highway, and into the history of a generation that is not mine. Surely that is why the women a decade younger than me get all the jobs I would like. They read Sally.

I phoned my sister after writing that last paragraph, one I thought would be a nice flattering ending for my baby-boomer readers: boomers as the free-spirits we war babies could never be. I asked her about Sally.

She ruminated about her first years of school, only eight months of them spent in Newfoundland. She remembers being so proud, "arrogant" she calls it, that when she went to Carpathia Road School in Winnipeg for grade one, she could already read and the other kids could not. This was the result of our no-nonsense Newfoundland education; we were way ahead of the prairie kids, but lost out in the end because they laughed at our Newfoundland accents and we felt inferior. But Kathy had no memory of Sally. I described Sally's exploits. No, that kind of girl Kathy would have remembered. She remembers Dick and Jane and *little* Sally and their dog Spot, she remembers all sorts of animal heroes, and of course she remembers television, not a factor in my formative years, but no adventurous Sally tripping off around the world.

After the phone call I checked my copy of the Newfoundland curriculum again. I discovered that when Sally entered the curriculum, it was not under the guise of reading, but listed under "Social Studies, optional." I laughed out loud. A term like social studies never entered my childhood school life. I see the point now. It wasn't Sally that was important, it was the places she went. Students were supposed to learn about the urban infrastructure from all those fire stations and postal depots, supposed to learn geography from all those visits to palm trees and pines.

It seems that Eleanor Thomas was subversive as well as clever, making little Sally into a person under the guise of "Social Studies." I must watch out for such women writers in the old curriculum material, though I doubt if the classrooms of my childhood would have much to do with that sort of thing. We were far too busy memorizing and worshipping the kings of England, contrarily brushing up Newfoundland pride with history books that scolded England for their bad treatment and neglect of us, and getting our noses into books that confusingly introduced us to the new mythology of Canadian nationalism that seemed to offer centre stage to those same Frenchmen who once pillaged and burned the homes of my ancestors. Past grade three, that is past 1948, the year of our confederation with Canada, the politics of school, indeed of life, got a lot more complex, and something like a Sally was the last thing on the agenda of my school system beyond those early grades. But that's another story. Working in the collection of curriculum memorabilia at Memorial University, I was grateful to even have found Sally. I think I'll adopt her as a kind of replacement for Mary Lou. Nurtured properly, Sally is bound to be good for my writing.

History and Politics: My Brother Dave, His Friend Sid and Louis St. Laurent

An event that happened in the city of St. John's in Newfoundland in 1948 repeats itself in my memory like a throb, a breath, as if there is something for me to know now, almost fifty years later, about two small boys—my brother Dave and his friend Sid—and the great man from the mainland who had come to tell us it was a very good idea for us Newfoundlanders to become Canadians.

I know how to tend to these memories of my girlhood now, when they take me over like this, repeating, insistent, as visually sharp as this evening's Florida sunset. They wake me at night and demand attention. I am into revision; half a century makes you do that. When I can't make the repetitions stop, then I have to dig at the memory with words, fill it up with plot and narrative and characters, and make sense of it.

My brother Dave and his friend Sid are standing on the curb in front of our house on Craigmillar Avenue. Since I was seven that year, they must have been ten, or perhaps Sid was older. The big, black limousine is coming down our avenue toward the centre of the small, old city of St. John's, bringing its precious cargo, the Prime Minister of Canada. It comes very slowly, and slows even more as it nears Dave and Sid. It is going to stop. It does stop. And in a kind of slow motion dream sequence like you see in old movies, the kind of movies they had when I was seven, the car stops, the door opens (or was it only the window?), the great man puts out his hand, pats each boy on the head and speaks. My dream sequence has no words so I cannot tell you what he said.

I know now that when you have waking dreams like this, memory reels, repeating again and again like something out of a Margaret

Laurence novel, then—as any decent therapist or writer will tell you—you have made a prism into the past-self which is inviting you to turn it over and see how much light it can catch. You have to look through the glass of Dave and Sid, through the great Louis St. Laurent himself—putting his hand out and ever so tenderly, ever so avuncularly, patting the boys' heads. These images from history are only the glass though which to see the self. What matters here is not the boys or the man, but you, or rather me, the younger sister of Dave who is standing, not on the curb beside the boys, but a few feet back, close to the white picket fence with the ornate brick and concrete posts that our father built.

Why is Helen Margaret—the willful, determined believer in her own brilliance that I have been telling you about—not right in there with the boys, getting her head patted, receiving the blessing of the great man? I want to try out three reasons on you, just for the purposes of getting on with the story: (1) By now Helen has learned her place, behind the boys, the great man being far too grand a personage for her to greet; or (2) by now Helen is very, very careful about the possibility of any adult male touching any part of her; or (3) wise little Helen knows the blessing would not really be a benefit, since she does not live in these male plots. The answer, I will tell you before we start, is all of the above and more.

At any rate, it was an amazing day. Our part of Craigmillar Avenue, full of citizens opposed to confederation with Canada, pulled its shades and closed its doors to Canada's leader. Mother, to show our passionate confederate stand, but not too brazenly, stood on the front steps with little Hal, while David, his friend Sid and Helen (a few feet behind) were allowed to stand by the roadside for their moment in history.

In fact, history was very much in my mind that year, for David was beginning to have real history books in school, books I yearned for and would soon have too. There would be *The Story of England and the Empire, The Story of Newfoundland* (later changed to add Labrador to its title), and eventually, when the great men did their work of confederation, I would arrive in grade six to have my very own, *Story Workbook in Canadian History*, the first spiral-spined book I had ever owned. I really owned it, since I wrote my answers dutifully on the dotted lines provided at the ends of chapters. This book would pass on to no other child. It was like my own personal Canadian citizenship papers, sent by Uncle Louie, whose touch I had failed to receive when he came in person.

The *Story Workbook* taught me that the history of New France was my history also, that Cartier, Champlain, and the Jesuits at Long Sault were all mine. This concept had to be held inside my head with the opposite idea that, as obviously illustrated by *The Story of Newfoundland*, the French were our sworn enemy, the armed raiders that were hellbent on killing my ancestors. But that little problem had been resolved when Sir Wilfrid Laurier went to London for Queen Victoria's jubilee and everyone there loved him so much—Canada's first French Prime Minister—that the Queen made him a "sir." This was a happy ending, because the spiral-spined book explained that all the bad stuff was past: "Once French and English had fought each other for possession of Canada, and more than once French-speaking and English-speaking Canadians had quarrelled bitterly." This I knew because of my own family's history in Carbonear, and because I'd also heard that some priests in Newfoundland had preached to the Catholics during the confederation debate, telling them not to vote for Canada or they would be ruled by a French archbishop from Quebec. But as the book reassured me, "all that was now forgotten." And so I filled in my dotted line answers with no conscious twinge of my false position: Question: "What phrase is often used to describe the years during which Sir Wilfrid Laurier was Prime Minister of Canada?" Answer: "the Golden Age of Sir Wilfrid Laurier." Question: "Tell in your own words why the people of London gave Sir Wilfrid Laurier such a warm welcome in 1897." I loved the "in your own words" answers, so I wrote: "Because they were overjoyed that Canada had a French prime minister and French and English would never fight again, not even in Newfoundland."

Of course this wasn't the first time I had to accept that history made contraries into smooth unity. After all, the *Story of Newfoundland* told me, again and again, that the English were very neglectful of their first colony. They just didn't seem to take their responsibilities seriously. Newfoundlanders were constantly sending home appeals for help with the various disorders; the English would send some decent fellow like Sir Richard Whitbourne and he would set things straight and then he went home, and as the book observes repeatedly: "Unfortunately when he left, no one was sent to replace him, and matters soon became as bad as ever." As bad as ever meant that a bunch of fishing admirals from the southwest of England got to pass laws that prohibited cultivation of the land or even the erection of buildings, except when required by the fisheries, and it took a hundred years to get things on a proper footing. It was hard to put all this together with the beneficent Mother England that was portrayed in *The Story of England and the Empire*, but maybe Newfoundland had just been a place to practice on, and indeed England must have learned to do better eventually because the map of the world in our classrooms showed just about everything had turned pink, the colour of the Empire, the empire on which the sun never set.

The U.S.A. must also have been a practice colony too, because this year as we drove through the old colonies on the way to sunny Florida and I read the brief histories in our guidebooks aloud to Richard as we went, we noted that these texts always start with the sins of the British. Did you know that Georgia was never really a slave state? It was made a slave territory by the British, and it seems that once these nasties were driven out with the revolution, the light was seen immediately and Georgians just worked like crazy to get rid of this ugly stain on their reputation.

History has to turn big, hard corners everywhere, but in Newfoundland it had to go round in circles seeking to make everybody all right. Even the United States. By the time I spent my last school year in Newfoundland, grade nine in 1954 (just before we emigrated to the Prairies), my history book, *The Great Adventure*, was telling me that the Americans were wonderful because they had invented the Marshall Plan which gave "over five billion dollars to the war-damaged countries of Europe." These were the same Americans that occupied the military bases in Newfoundland, who often, it was hinted, debauched Newfoundland girls (whatever that meant) or took them away to who knows what fates in America. History was getting harder and harder.

History worked its way around all this confusion and finally came up with a correct story that went something like this: Newfoundlanders were a strong and free people who, with little help from anyone, had achieved one hundred years of independence which had to be given up because of some hard-to-understand money matters. We came again under the wicked rule of the Colonial Office. Now, however, we did not need independence or money, because we would be part of the great Canadian nation where the French were no longer our enemy, a sea-to-sea nation which had showed those pushy manifest-destiny, slave-owning Americans a thing or two in the War of 1812. These Americans were obviously morally a rank or two below us because they had wimped out on the League of Nations and weren't even good enough to be part of the British Empire which had started, my history book said, at the time of the Romans and marched forward through history to this wonderful moment when we were turning into the Commonwealth where all of us would be safe and free under the rule of law, and we could easily forget that the same people who had made those laws had also run the wicked old Colonial Office.

Not only that, it seemed just about everything now depended on Canada (which now meant Newfoundland too) behaving properly, since, as my history book put it, America and Britain "were friends, yet they did not understand each other very well. But they both trusted Canada. She had grown up between them and she understood them both; she explained each of them to the other. In Canada, Britain saw a United States that she could understand and like. In Canada the United States saw a Britain that she could understand and like. Canada was a strong link between these two great powers and a friendly link between them and the smaller nations. She was a 'Middle Power.'" As *The Great Adventure* observes: "This is an important and difficult position."

The Great Adventure was not telling me anything I did not already know at some level. I think even then I must have had some inkling that whenever they tell you that you are serving an "important and difficult" function, it's usually because you're wondering if you have any power at all and you feel like you are about to get caught in the middle. I like to think that I already knew, underneath my gullible surface of smooth-as-skin acceptance of the ideology of nationhood, that Canada was a "she" in these sentences for very good reasons. You see, in my own "great adventure," as a little girl, history always eventually turned to politics and where there is politics there is always sex. Or as we more correctly say today, gender.

But the truth is, those tender years were long before I knew how to be so cynical; it was long before the word "bullshit" was to become, not the battle cry, but the snarled undertone of a generation born when the Russians were our brothers in the fight against the evil Germans, but who grew up to find the Germans our hard-working entrepreneurial partners and the Russians the threatening hordes behind the iron curtain. Everywhere history talked with forked tongue. What's a girl to do?

What this girl actually did, was to invent her own story of the world. It begins with Boadicea, Queen of the Britons. I have a vivid memory—one of those that is so lifelike in its three-dimensional, statue-like hardness that you can almost touch it—of me at my grade five desk with *The Story of England and the Empire* open at her picture. She stands windblown in her chariot, her long red hair flaming with resistance, her taut muscular left arm wrapped around the reins that hold the heads of her powerful team of madly charging steeds. In her right hand she aims her spear, powerfully, accurately toward the Romans, who fall away before her, shields cast aside, eyes wild with fear, their deaths near. Her eyes are absolutely steady, not a flicker of anything but pure will, honed and aimed, the righteousness of a woman protecting her people. Each day, as we tiny history students worked our way through the boring details of the War of the Roses and memorized the Plantagenet kings, I would sneak looks back at Boadicea on her chariot.

At this moment in time, as I examine page thirty-one of *The Story of England and the Empire*, I realize that memory has been busy going about its revisionary work. I had never noticed there is a dead man in the foreground of the picture. Maybe he's a Roman whom Boadicea has just slaughtered, but he could well be a Briton; I see that the Romans are not fleeing, but have their shields firmly in place in front of their bodies, their spears nicely aimed at Her Majesty. She, on the other hand is not alone, but accompanied by at least one other standing figure, who may or may not be a woman, and . . . damn it! I take off my glasses to examine the picture up close, right eye shut to let my dominant eye catch the detail. There are two men hiding in that wagon! One seems to have his hands on the reins, the other is crouched in front of the queen, obviously preparing to receive the blows meant for her. Boadicea herself seems rather casual, less than intense, and worst of all she is downright pretty! Her right hand, holding a very small, toylike sword, is limply cast off to the side as if she's tentatively wondering whether she should drop her tiny weapon over the edge of the chariot. I cannot tell if her hair is red as I have always remembered it; the picture is a black and white sketch.

I'm almost afraid to read the text which reminds me of what I have conveniently suppressed: Boadicia drank poison rather than be sent a prisoner to Rome. What I had forgotten entirely was that history makes Boadicia share the spotlight with some guy called Caractacus who was also a defeated Briton, or more accurately, a Welshman. He did go to Rome, behaved so nobly, or perhaps Welsh-like, that the Roman emperor gave him his freedom again. Of course he never showed his face back home. I like Boadicia's poisonous solution. It puts her in the martyr league with one of my other heroines, Joan of Arc, who really is pictured nobly by my history book. Sitting astride a giant, rearing horse, clothed in her full armour and carrying her battle flag, she leads her soldiers, all of them properly placed to her rear, as they face what looks like some sharpened logs and a dreadful horde of Englishmen.

It was about this time that *The Story of England and the Empire* started to turn those tough corners. Joan was obviously the heroine, and the English, my people, were not. The book tries to tell it simply: "Then a shameful thing happened. The Maid of Orléans was captured and handed over to the English. She was accused of being a witch, and was burnt to death in the marketplace of Rouen." I remember this terrible betrayal used to bother me a lot. I found it hard to decide where my loyalties lay. The French obviously should have looked after the Maid more carefully, but the English were worse; that could not be argued away. I concentrated my attention on the word shameful, calling up all the shameful things I could think of to try to assess what my history book was telling me.

Shameful was a strong word. In *The Story of Newfoundland*, when it told of the belated attempts to save the last of the aboriginal people of Newfoundland, the Beothucks—of how Shanawdithit, in captivity, drew pictures of caribou, counted on her fingers the handful of her race she believed to be still alive, while she coughed out her life in consumption—the *Story* said that this was "one of the saddest chapters in the history of British colonization." While the death of Joan was shameful, the death of a people was not shameful, merely sad. I was concerned with the difference between sadness and shame.

I didn't know then that the choice of shame or sadness might have to do with the politics of race or just mere numbers of dead: one death of a white person traceable to one or two easily knowable causes was shameful, many deaths of aboriginals having multiple perpetrators and multiple causes became merely sad. From inside my life it seemed that sadness was what I felt when a stray cat was found in our basement and we kids wanted to keep it as a pet and our mother told us that animals did not belong in houses with humans, and besides our father did not like pets, and we would not be able to keep it. The cat had held my eyes and I had held hers. I was sad when she was gone, sad for a long time, but eventually not sad. Shame on the other hand was what I felt when the father of the boys next door walked up to me while I was skipping and put his hands between my legs, pinching me where I peed. Shame was the feeling that something terribly wrong had happened, something deeply forbidden, something you did not dare tell your parents about, because it was bound to be your fault, because wasn't any occasion where you said an adult did something wrong always your fault? Shame like that would never go away. Like the flames licking at Joan's feet, it would stay forever in your head, a steely implant that scraped and pierced the soft tissues of your brain now and then, at times you least expect it. Like now.

It seems obvious to me as an adult feminist that what I should have been feeling then was neither shame nor sadness at the fates of my heroines. What I should have felt was robbed: robbed of a fuller history, robbed of the very moral values my culture told me it abided by. But that's easy from here. Now I have my own beliefs, beliefs wrung out of the guts of my own experience at great cost to little Helen Margaret. Then I had only what my family, my school and my church were willing to let me have. And they kept breaking their own rules and I didn't like to admit that they did. I think, looking back, that was the reason for making my own stories. I could sidestep the issues, suppress the sadness and shame, not feel a part of a shameful world, mired in sadness. So it is that I have this very clear memory of my rescue of Shanawdithit.

In my fantasy I am the daughter of W.E. Cormack who founded the Beothuck Institute in St. John's in 1827. My worthy father is desperately trying to learn more about the native people of Newfoundland, in an effort to contact them and save the ones left from the murderous behaviours of former times. He brings Shanawdithit from where she has been living for five years with the Peytons in the settlement of Exploits to St. John's, and she lives in our home, draws beautiful pictures, and becomes my friend. I am the only one who calls her Shanawdithit; everyone else calls her Nancy. When she becomes ill with consumption, she begs me to help her escape. I do. Off we go, into the wilderness. There are various versions of this. The escape plots get quite complex. Imagine a few yourself. They will all fit. I used to like the learning-to-survive-in-the-wilderness plots the best: how Shanawdithit teaches me to use snowshoes and chew deerskins until they are soft leather and how I brew up a secret tea that my grandmother taught me to make on the Scottish moors, tea which cures Shanawdithit's illness. (It was necessary to invent a Scottish grandmother to get a proper Celtic ancestor, in touch with the ways of the old Britons, those never conquered by Rome.) We live in a teepee of course and hunt in the winter and live off berries in the summer, and swim as early as we want in the spring brooks, not waiting until summer holidays. Every day is a holiday for me and Shanawdithit. We are always just the two of us. In my stories we never seem to make much effort to find her people or mine. We live outside of history. We have no sadness nor shame. Of course, nowadays I realize that this fantasy is merely an appropriation of someone else's tragedy, honed into story to make me feel less shame. I know I have no right to make such a story, that I have to live with sadness and shame as part of my share of history. But then, when I was a child, I had an escape route. And like every other white person, I wish I had one now.

Fortunately, one figure in my selected history of the Empire is above such fleshy complexities as sadness and shame. She is the first Queen Elizabeth. And what a survivor she is! The constancy of her image in my personal childhood museum of heroines is an act of survivorship, because all of Western ideology has been working hard for the last fifty years or so, trying to destroy her. But she has survived inside my memory, when all others, including the second Elizabeth, have been brought low. The myth-makers of History and Hollywood have tried to convince me that she was a vicious old bitch who killed her own cousin out of spite, that she was a dried up old hag who couldn't get a man to love her, that she was gulled and betrayed and bald! The postcolonials even want to convince me that she's the one where the shame and blame of empire starts. But they can't get at her either. She is safe with me. Inside my memory museum she is still the beautiful woman in robes of splendour, riding through London on her horse as all about her the people cheer. So what if the picture in the *Story* shows her horse held by a page and herself closely guarded by soldiers.

For me she is the queen inside myself, and no matter how hard history or the movies try to tear her out by the roots, she's not leaving. She sits imperious and watchful as a hawk inside my head, alert to the smallest sign of anything less than complete loyalty, knowing that you are either on top or you simply are not anywhere. The political incorrectness of this condition makes me cackle with laughter inside my corrupt psyche, for I know that despite the fact that we feminists must be egalitarian to have any kind of consistent philosophy, there is part of me that wants power, real power to keep going in a hostile world. If some of us occasionally act like Maggie Thatcher, well, just try walking in our shoes for a day or two. Some days it would be so much easier to just be better at all the things men in power do, rather than doing the hard work of becoming a woman who is not a slave. Mimicry is so much easier than making a new kind of person.

So the *Story* of the empire offers me Elizabeth as an example of a female who ruled. It says that "in those days almost everyone thought that, if a country had a queen, it was not the queen who *really* ruled. It might be the queen's husband, or her nephew, or a great minister, who was the real ruler—but it certainly could not be the queen herself. No one believed that a woman could rule in the same way as a man—but Queen Elizabeth proved them all wrong. For forty-five years she ruled England as well, as wisely and as firmly as any king could have done." And so it was with little Helen Margaret. Whoever seems to be in charge on the outside, it is her queenly self that is on the throne, remaking reality to suit herself.

Speaking of stories, I just looked at the title page of *The Story of England and the Empire*. It was written by John Mackenzie Wood, M.A., "Sometime Scholar of Clare College, Cambridge," and Aileen Garland, B.A., Principal, William White School, Winnipeg. Can you guess who put the above judgment on Elizabeth into the *Story*? I'd wager my membership in the women's movement that anyone who could run William Whyte School in Winnipeg also had a bit of Queen Elizabeth in her head too, and knew how to write about it. She would certainly understand how important it was for the young queen "to insist on her orders being obeyed"; she would know full well what it was like to sit on a throne "alone and almost friendless"; she would know how important music and singing and poetry and plays are to a people's identity, just as Elizabeth did, and she would feel the same pride and yearning when she sent those young men off in ships to find their new worlds. I am sure that the world which Queen Aileen ran in Winnipeg was just like the Elizabethan one she describes: "Such was the England that obeyed Elizabeth. It was cheerful, brave, high-hearted; and it was freer and happier than England had been for many years." I've been told that the Greeks used to get all shaky and wilted when they thought of the barbaric ages of their past, when men knew no better than to obey their mothers. What a grand time that must have been, when people like Queen Elizabeth I and Eileen Garland, B.A., ruled the earth!

There, I have told you the truth of how I perverted history with the help of my subversive foremother, Aileen Garland, B.A. I would like to leave it at that, but of course, the record of history will not let me. For while Queen Elizabeth inhabits me as much as Virginia Woolf does, and both need my constant vigilance and protection, we have a history inside this body that is as important as empires, as difficult to write as is literature. One of the hardest times for all three of us, as you might expect, was puberty. I don't know if you've noticed, but puberty does not begin for a little girl in this culture when hormonal changes bring her body to fertility. Try to imagine a situation in which girls are not subjected to any sexual pressures until the blood flow begins, and then they get to have neat ceremonies with other women, rituals which let them know that this amazing change gives them status, value, both for themselves and in the greater world of adult women. A bit like me imagining I lived in the wilderness with the last of the Beothucks.

Puberty is not a physical fact so much as it is a political fact. In today's world puberty begins with the assault of a sex-drenched, reproductively starved ideology mounting a little girl's mind with masochistic images of her body as object of desire. In my day things worked a little differently. No television existed to shape our imaginary selves, but instead we had the hands of men protected by the terrible positivism of a society that said all dads were good guys. They were not, but this method of intimidation worked as well as the present moment's pornography of mass-media advertisement.

I see that I'm starting to go off on one of my feminist ideological rambles. It is Virginia's anger and good Queen Bess's need to make policy statements that is making me do it. I've avoided my word processor for a few days now, as it has begun to dawn on me that I can't really write the history of sexual politics in my small childhood world without writing about the personal incidents and attitudes that informed my coming of age. I've walked on this Florida beach and sat by the water letting the pull and push of the ocean drown out thought, hoping that at the end of an hour of unselfconsciousness I might find some other way to work words, besides this crass confession. Each time I went to the water I was soothed by the rhythms; each time the water released me, the same hard, dangerous consciousness returned. For that's what it is really about: a violent coming to consciousness. With a little luck, a child in my time, because of the blessed lack of today's screaming, tortured mass-media sexuality, could grow quite a few years being unselfconscious of her body as a site of sexual exploitation. It meant that I could navigate the strictures of my ideology regarding female gendering by simply ignoring my body. Gender training could be tuned out in the pre-multimedia world I lived in. Deep in my imagination, my body hardly existed, except for brief moments when my mother made me clean it.

But my luck ended when I was eleven. The family for whom I baby-sat at that tender age would seem to have been an ideal one: a pretty mother, the father a steady worker, a beautiful little daughter just past infancy. The parents liked to go out in the evening to play cards at the neighbours. I suppose my mother thought this was the safest kind of childcare I could do, with the parents a mere phone call away. Besides, my mother must have thought I was already well trained as a child-minder. My little sister Kathy had been born three years before and at times I was assigned the job of taking her for walks in her baby carriage. Despite my love of dolls with real hair, I did not have any maternal feelings for little Kathy, resented taking her on my perambulations through the neighbourhood, practiced bouncing her pram over such rough ground that her wide eyes almost popped. I even occasionally experimented with wondering how fast a pram might travel down the slope of Craigmillar Avenue, just where it joined Topsail Road.

I tell you about my feelings for my baby sister not just because I would like to stave off starting this narration, but to illustrate that nothing in what is to follow put me off babies; I was already off them. I really liked the young mother of the baby; I hardly remember the little girl. The mother was more dress-conscious than my mother; she wore very high heels, her hair was carefully crafted, and she wore swirling, crinolined skirts before they became de rigeur for evenings out. I liked the fact that she was never ready to leave when I arrived. Her husband would apologize and laugh while she occasionally came sweeping through the hallway outside the living room where I sat, rushing between some household detail and her mysterious beauty routines. I would follow her with hungry, curious eyes.

I took to wearing my nicest clothes when I went there, because she always commented on my appearance. Simple compliments like, "Your hair has such a nice gleam to it. What do you use for shampoo?" I had no idea what my mother insisted I wash my hair with during my Saturday bath, but I was thrilled with the notice, as nobody had ever said anything nice about my brownish, straight, thin hair. On my second or third visit to her home I deliberately wore my twin-sweater set, received for Christmas and to be worn only for church and special occasions (we wore uniforms at school). I carefully pinned on my little bumblebee brooch, the one with the golden jewel in the place of the bumblebee's body. Attached to the bumblebee by two little golden-coloured chains were two baby bumblebees. I loved this, because you could choose where to put the babies, in front, behind, or below the mother bumblebee. This night I looped the two babies high above their mother, like balloons coming up from behind her as she flew. Walking to her home I wondered what the beautiful young mother would say. I knew she loved bright colours and my bumblebees were a very bright amber colour, as bright as the purple and green satins she wore and shiny as the amazing shawl with silver threads running through it that she had once thrown around her shoulders as she smiled at me and swished out the door.

This time when I arrived, she was upstairs putting her little girl to bed. The husband greeted me, took my coat and I went into the living room, as usual, with my pile of homework. I was sitting reading one of my books when he arrived in front of me. He bent down, and took the body of the mother bumble bee in his fingers and said, close to my ear, "What a pretty little brooch. Is it a bumblebee?"

"Yes," I said.

Look at that "yes" with its three little letters sitting there all by itself. Hardly a thing to cause shame for a lifetime. But it has. Despite all the ways in which we women have learned in these recent years to validate our own innocence in these dreadful scenarios, in my head I still live in a 1950s world where that simple "yes" makes me culpable. I'm still trying to figure out why I feel that way. I think its a bit like the proverbial child in the room alone. If a teacup falls, she feels she must have done it, because nothing is causeless, everything has something to do with you, the child at the centre of the universe. Maybe it has to do with dads all being good, and if anybody is doing something wrong here, it cannot be a dad. Maybe it was a reasoning I made as an extension of the rule that in any difference between adult and child, the adult is right. This was always the way it was when we tried to complain about a teacher. Even though my grade three teacher seemed to very obviously work at making me cry about my spelling so that she could hold me up as a bad example before other kids, my parents firmly let me know that there was no defence in a quarrel with an authority figure. You were wrong, they were right. Try learning to spell better.

That first time, he merely brushed his fingers across the place, just below the bumblebee pin, where my left breast would be in about two years. But soon a terrible game began. Each time I arrived to baby-sit, he would find excuses to come in the living room while his wife was elsewhere. I remember he always moved quickly, purposefully. As soon as I saw him coming, I would go stiff, pull a book toward me, pretend to read. Sometimes he would just pick up an ashtray and go out, sometimes he would grab his tie from where he had left it, just behind my chair, hung from the lamp shade. My whole body would come alive with fear, with the desire to flee; but no, not flee: my whole body became absolutely electrified with a current that kept me completely still, unmoving. He would leave the room and I would think: There, you imagined what happened last time. Then suddenly he would be there, rubbing his fingers across my sweater or blouse where my nipples must have been or putting his hands on the knees of my black school stockings, and fingering up my legs.

Soon my frozen passivity gave way to a kind of silent stiff struggle. My book would slam against my chest as he reached for me, my legs would twist around themselves as his hand slid upward. I found that I had to draw my knees up toward my stomach to keep his hand from travelling up toward the place where I peed. And all the time I sat in the same chair, not daring to flee, for fleeing would mean having to tell, and telling would mean blame. This was not like when I was six and the dad next door touched me. I was a child then, more mobile, more able to find safety in numbers. Now, in the pre-teen solitude of the baby-sitter's workplace, I had no place to run.

And he got smarter. He would leave me alone in my silent fear as his wife got ready upstairs. When she arrived, beautiful in chartreuse or pink, I would practically shiver with relief. Now they would go out, now I would be safe. Then, just as they went out the door, back he would come for something he forgot, and the terrible stiff struggle would go another round.

One night, when they were playing cards directly across the street, he came home early, and announced that his wife had sent him ahead to walk me home, and would send along my pay tomorrow. The wife, not he, always paid me. I rushed toward the closet where my coat was, two steps up the landing of the stairs. He caught me on the first step, sat himself down on the landing and pulled me to his lap. He started whispering as he felt me: "If you're afraid of my wife, don't worry, I won't tell her. It's all right. She'll never know. It's all right." It is only at this moment, as I write this through its third revision—trying for less reticence—that I realize the way in which he concocted our complicity, the way he assumed his desire was also mine! While he whispered, one hand went under my sweater, and the other up under my skirt. Under my sweater I still wore the sort of childhood undershirts that I had worn since grade one; they had a full, tight bodice with sleeves and little straps at the end of them, straps that slide beneath your thick woolen underpants and down your legs to hold up the tops of your stockings. Under my sweater he would have a hard time finding any flesh. But between my underpants and the tops of my stockings, there was a space of flesh which I have been told is now regularly fetishized in soft-porn movies. In that space, if you had a mind to, you could find my skinny little eleven-year-old thighs. He obviously had a mind to. This was the first time he had actually managed to touch my flesh. I don't even remember what it felt like but I knew this was too much. This had something to do with getting pregnant. My panic took me away from him and somehow out the door with books and coat within seconds, where I met his wife coming up the walk.

"Wait, wait, Helen, I haven't paid you. Helen, I promised your mother we would walk you home." She called to her husband to walk me to my house.

He caught up to me, whispering, "Slow down, slow down." I did not slow down. Then the most dreadful thing happened. He started to apologize. "I'm sorry. Did I hurt you? I'm sorry. You won't tell will you? You won't tell will you?"

It is hard to describe the extent of my disgust and horror. I hated this man. Not just because of the touching. I felt an awful physical disgust for this voice that apologized, that begged me not to tell. Something in me understood and accepted the abuse of power; except for the sexual content, that was almost ordinary; hadn't I learned that lesson in school, everywhere? The powerful often misuse their power. They are bullies. A fact of life. It was this apologizing and pleading that I truly hated, that made me want to throw up. He was pretending he was like me: frightened, helpless, at the mercy of someone else. Pretending that we were equals. That somehow I, a child, had some power here. This apology of his, this pleading—did he think it absolved him, did he think it made him a good man, made me the bad girl?—this was truly obscene. I felt it right down to my gut.

Well, he wasn't like me. He was a monster. I ran ahead of his voice, answering his repeated, "Please don't tell" only as I got close enough to home to feel safe. Despite the turmoil in my gut and my heart and my mind, I also instinctively knew that there was no way out, except to make a deal with him: "Don't come near me. I won't tell, but don't you come near me." It was an easy promise to make. I would not dare risk being blamed for this by telling.

I never went to their house again. When my mother told me I was wanted there for baby-sitting, I said I didn't like baby-sitting and I would not go. When she inquired further, I went into one of my usual cranky sulks, saying I hated baby-sitting, hated babies, didn't care about the money, any answer that would get her off my back. My mother was disturbed enough about my attitude to tell my father. When I answered him with as surly a rejection as I had given her, he said I was going through a phase, and Kathleen should know by now that there was no point trying to make Helen do something when she didn't want to. "You know how she will get." Mother tried once more. She told me how Mrs. _____ was very hurt that I wouldn't come. She had sent me two dollars, much more than the $1.25 she owed me for five hours of baby-sitting. I can see the two dollar bills rolled in my mother's hand as clearly today as if it were over four decades ago. My mother asked me how I could be so selfish as to refuse to baby-sit for this generous woman? I don't know what I said to my mother, but whatever it was, it was a lie, and she left me alone.

When I was in my forties and Mother and I were talking about some of the characters in the old neighbourhood, I let slip that the man next door used to try to feel me up when I was about six. Mother reasoned that I must have imagined it. My older brother David was with us at the time and mentioned that he had heard about this man's behaviour from one of the other neighbourhood girls, a girl his age. My mother believed my brother. I don't know if she believed him because he was my brother or merely because he offered collaborating evidence from an older girl, but I find it interesting that my reputation for an active imagination still carries with it the penalty of being an unreliable witness. I did not bother to tell her about the baby-sitting experience; I couldn't count on my brother knowing about more than one neighbourhood hazard for pre-pubescent girls.

Reading what I have written about this molestation in this moment of third revision, I begin to realize how lucky I was. In accepting my surly refusal to return, my parents accepted my right to refuse. My only wish is that I could have gotten my way in life without resorting to petulant anger. As it is, it's taken me most of my adulthood to find that sometimes more measured responses can work.

When I look back now I realize that the hardest part of the experience was not anything I have told you, but the terror of the months that followed. I don't suppose an eleven-year-old girl of today could be so ignorant as to believe that a man's touch on the skin of her upper thigh could make her pregnant. But I did. I can remember very clearly feeling my abdomen each night in bed, trying to decide if it was larger. Sometimes, after a good meal, it was. I would cry with fear thinking about what my parents would do to me if I were pregnant. I would have to kill myself to avoid telling them. When I figured enough time had passed that I had escaped pregnancy, I became very careful about things having to do with my body. I insisted on a locked bathroom door. I was careful never to sit by boys or men on streetcars and buses, and gave them a wide berth passing in the street. I was very careful not to look at my body when I dressed or undressed.

This incident, along with my experience at two years old when my father was taken away from me by war and the later experience of being kicked out of the boys' club, are the three historical markers that my adult psyche has chosen as its making moments. Sort of like Magna Carta, the Spanish Armada and Waterloo, or the landing of the *Mayflower*, the Boston Tea Party, and the Gettysburg Address, or Cabot's discovery of North America and . . . well Canadians would disagree on any series of marker events. But like national identity, personal identity makes itself on moments that in retrospect mark a great change, ones that set the course of the future sense of the self and reality.

When I was two and lost my father forever, as far as my little psyche could understand, I became the divided self that I think is fairly common in my world, in my age group. It's not just the loss that makes the split; it is also the insistence of our culture that a father going to war is not to be seen as causing the same effect that any split of the child's coupled universe might cause—say the death of a parent, or a divorce. The cultural assumption that there is no need to wildly howl against the injustice of such a loss eventually stills the cries of even the most traumatized child into a careful obedience. But just below the surface of this polite, civilized child is a maelstrom of grief and anger. Any event that imitates the original trauma, any minor desertion, any small silencing, can throw the main switch of power and repeat the emotion of the original event. It can still happen to me today; without warning I am a sobbing heap of uncontrollable tears. Sometimes the betrayals that throw the switch are small; sometimes they do indeed almost measure up to the first loss.

When I was six or seven I was made aware that I was capable of taking up an axe to right an injustice. I truly have felt, on many occasions, the urge to kill those who take up their gender power with so little thought of its price. I have had to be very careful about this intense talent, working a lifetime to hone the axe into words.

And when I was eleven, I learned my third lesson of civilized identity: You do not need to live inside a body so powerless that anyone can use it. You can tend that body, use that body, eventually learn to protect that body, even, if you have a mind to, take pleasure from that body. But you do not have to live there. To this day I have a pretty high pain threshold; it takes my body quite a while to send messages to me that it is in pain. To this day I have to check my reflection in windows and mirrors that I pass to make sure I'm there, that everything checks out. For most of my adult life my body has tried to gain as much weight as it can to remind me of its existence, and I have responded by disciplining it in various ways, resisting, as best as I can, its cries for attention. I don't think I am untypical. If most of us lived in our bodies we would not put up with much of what passes for culture, all the ways in which we must experience life through secondary means. If we lived in our bodies we would not stand for all the ways in which we "postpone gratification," as the psycho-babble puts it. If we really lived in our bodies we wouldn't have to make such a big deal about orgasm. Orgasm, in our world, is the cheap and easy way we keep our bodies under the impression that we live in them. Of course, disease is making orgasm less easy and sometimes very expensive. Some days now, when I lose the optimism that I work hard to hold on to and the cynicism surges up, I feel that we are, as a culture—in the words of that massive generation just behind me—"totally fucked up."

And that is history too. And politics. When I analyze the babysitting incident from the distance of forty years and several kinds of educations in life and culture, I realize all sorts of lessons about the century I live in. There's a lot in it about my parents' class background. They were raised in a closely knit rural world and if there had been a child-molester down the road in their villages they would certainly have known about it. I suppose to this day it would be hard for them to believe that even in the city of St. John's they would not know. But then again, to be fair, they must have learned hard lessons as they grew older. I remember one occasion when as an adult and a mother myself, I visited my parents in their home outside Toronto, when my youngest was four. I was about to let him go with his nine-year-old sister to the playground a block away. My father told me I shouldn't be so trusting; there are some very weird people out there nowadays. He insisted he go along with them telling me I wasn't in my Winnipeg home now; this was the big city.

For a long time in my adulthood I blamed my parents for their ignorance of the dangers of my childhood world, for their insistence on the rightness of people in authority. When I look back now I realize that my parents had reactions typical of those moving out of their own rural, working class into the new, urban middle classes. Many of the people that lived around them, certainly the teachers at the rather expensive school they sent their children to, were not always the kind of people they had grown to know in childhood. They were people of some rank, people they had been taught to respect, and whom they, in turn, expected their children to respect. Like all of us, they believed that with the new knowledge we were gaining in the twentieth century, the old human illnesses would be left behind. Indeed, if we were conquering tuberculosis and cholera, if we could cure my ear infections in a twinkling with a shot of penicillin, then surely evil was dead too, and the diseases it spread dead also.

At least that's the impression I got when I studied the "health" books that were fast becoming part of the school curriculum in the 1950s. It will seem a perverse feminist logic for me to tell you that science bears part of the responsibility for the sexual abuse I experienced as a child, but stay with me on this one, I promise to make sense. Science came to us through the science and health books we studied in school, expensively made texts that had the best shiny paper and the sturdiest covers I had ever seen. Now here was something substantial and authoritative, full of wonderful photographs of scientists doing their jobs, even a woman scientist demonstrating how the common cold does its dirty work. These books came from the United States of America, which was, in all our minds in the late 1950s—despite our knee-jerk anti-Americanism caused by the presence of military bases on our territory—the home of all things progressive and scientific. The preface to my grade seven science text, *Understanding Our Environment*, tells our teachers in no uncertain terms what this text is for:

> The method of science is kept constantly before the pupil's attention. Establishment of facts through observation is presented in experimental studies as well as through text and narrative. The organization of facts into a body of knowledge, their interpretation in a generalization at the pupil's level, the use of such generalization in the interpretation of facts in a new situation, the framing and testing of hypotheses, receive attention at strategic positions. Solutions of problems by scientists illustrates the method in use, and guidance in solution of problems provides opportunity for its exercise.

And so I began to learn that nothing is real unless you can set up an experiment that makes it real. I could see that from the pictures. There they were, scientists with test tubes, soil samples, air samples, burning things and crushing things and breaking things. They also injected things and sprayed things. Our science books and health books met each other at the site of the human body, which was, of course, a thing also. I remember being fascinated with a picture in *The Healthy Home and Community*, of Vesalius, the father of modern anatomy, scalpel in hand, holding the arm of a cadaver. Unfortunately the rest of the body is covered with a sheet and I cannot see it. But his two helpers, rather serious-looking fellows, are staring at the sheet so intensely that I am invited to imagine the body, cold and white, awaiting the exploration of the great scientist. The book says that Vesalius "wanted to see and handle for himself all the parts of the human body and find out how they are made." And he did. And our health and science books are filled with ways that you can handle the human body. There are boys feeling each others arm muscles to test their strength, and children standing on weigh scales to measure their growth, dentists standing over willing little girls about to have their teeth worked on. "The dentist is one of the best friends a small child can make," says the caption. Particularly impressive is the section on how modern science defeated typhus, malaria and other plagues. One of the pictures shows some rather shabby-looking men and boys in Naples, Italy, who are having their clothing dusted with DDT at a "delousing station." Another shows an airplane being sterilized. A man in a gas mask is on a ladder by the airplane door, while another hands him a canister. A huge sign in front of them says "Danger Keep Away Fumigation with Deadly Gas." Another picture shows some men in a boat spraying a marshland with a hose full of poison. The text tells me that "spraying pools with powdered Paris green is another way of killing the wrigglers. The tiny particles of Paris green closely resemble the tiny green plants, called algae, in which the wrigglers feed. When the wrigglers eat this poison, they die quickly."

It was obvious you did not mess with science. My own questionings were half-hearted. I once showed my father a smoke-belching industrial chimney in my geography book—which claimed that it was illustrating the progress of industry: "Where does all the smoke go," I asked.

"It goes up in the air."

"But where does it go? I insisted, knowing by now that no matter ever disappears.

"It just dissipates, becomes part of the atmosphere, part of the clouds, the rain, the earth."

Dissipates. This word silenced me. I had studied the cycle of evaporation, condensation and rainfall. The cycle said nothing about all that smoke. However, dissipates seemed such a scientific word. I remained dissatisfied about dissipation, but since science and my father were not worried, it must be all right. But in the back of my mind were those men and boys from Naples. They didn't look very happy having that spray-wand going around their heads. I looked again. I wondered if they sprayed that stuff over all parts of their bodies. I wondered about the unmentioned; my efficient health books covered every part of the human body, except for one, so I wondered about the absent part. There are no genitals anywhere in the whole series of books. From the earliest grades with *Spick and Span* and *The Health Parade*, through *Growing Big and Tall*, and *Safety Every Day*, to *Helping the Body Do Its Work* and *The Healthy Home and Community*, there was nothing to tell me how to keep my genitals safe. It was as if, with all this probing and poking and measuring and feeding and watering and caring of bodies, that part did not exist. I wondered if Vesalius ever found it in his desire to handle every part of the human body?

So if that part of my body wasn't in the health books and wasn't in the science books, then it wasn't really there. This meant that what happened with those men in my neighbourhood did not really happen. Now if the man next door had put his grimy fingers in my mouth and grabbed my teeth, or if the man where I baby-sat had taken my thumb and bent it back against my wrist until I screamed with the pain and torture of it, I might have a case, something which could be demonstrated. As far as I could see I had no way to proceed. There was no way to ask the question, gather the materials, perform the procedure, make the observation and draw the conclusion. At the very best what was between my legs was not even at the stage of scientific investigation that atomic energy was.

Atomic energy was at least recognized to exist and my science book was asking questions about it. "Will atomic energy destroy our civilization? Will it destroy mankind? Why is it so terrible? Why is it feared?" Next to these and a dozen other questions about the dreadful splitting atom that the world had only recently brought to my attention was the picture of the naked back and right arm of a woman. Etched on her skin is a dreadful script of black scars. Her back is real. Science can prove that an atom bomb did it. I needed to get in the category of "real." Some dreadful, earth-shaking event like a bomb needed to prove that the unmentioned parts of my body were there, prove it to me and to all the world. Then maybe we could ask some questions about how I had been hurt and who had hurt me and why. Until then I had to agree with science that parts of me just did not exist.

Now, Kathleen and Harold Clarke may have raised a naïve child, but they did not raise her to be stupid. Somewhere along the line they had taught me to hedge my bets. If science was not to recognize the existence of my genitals, well that was unfortunate, but just in case they did exist I had to take some precautions. Precautions become a way of life, and indeed my formerly risk-taking girlhood was quickly learning to take very few chances in a world where your most historically real and politically complex experiences had no existence, where that man next door and that man up the street continued to go about their businesses, walk to the bus stop, drive their cars, be hailed by their neighbours with smiles and waves, and were called Dad by kids just like me. In such a world, almost anybody or anything could be dangerous.

A girl had to watch out. So it was all right for Dave and Sid to make their communion with the great Louis St. Laurent, but I knew I was not them. Dave's embarrassing days of having his little sister stand out in the road and dare the neighbourhood bullies, simply because she didn't understand the sexual politics of turf only belonging to boys—that a girl's claim merely confused the issue, created a delay in proceedings— well, those days were over. I had certainly been taught my place this time, and just in time, considering that the hardest part was about to start, those dreadful years when a girl, any girl, despite the silence of the whole world, learns that she lives in a female body.

I have to tell you that not the entire world was silent, although it was trying hard to be. I remember when I was agonizing over the fact that some girls in my class had teased me because they had all started their "periods" and I had not (being a year younger than all of them, this is not surprising), I let slip to my friend Eleanor that although I knew what periods were when they were at the end of sentences, I didn't know what non-grammatical periods were. Eleanor had that look on her face that said she did know. Never being one to tolerate not knowing something someone else did, I began a campaign to find out what she knew. She resisted for a while, explaining that it was information that her mother had told her on the condition that it go no further. This merely drove my desire to know like a whip. Soon I had her breaking her promise to her mother. Her careful, and very scientific explanation of ovulation, the building of the site of conception, and the conditions of shedding of the uterine lining was like manna from heaven in a starved world: this was the most exciting and liberating science I had ever heard. Merely a year before I had thought a man's touch could make me pregnant, and now I learned that there was this complex process involved. If Eleanor's mother's science was correct, and I had no reason to doubt it, Eleanor's mother not being known to be a flighty or reckless woman, then all I had to do was avoid penises getting up this birth canal place which Eleanor assured me was somewhere between the place where I peed and the place where I pooped. As we walked up the steep part of Topsail Road just before it gets to Craigmillar Avenue, pushing our bikes, me absorbing this new and vital knowledge, Eleanor made me vow on my life that I would tell no one what she had told me. It's been over forty years since that day, so I'm hoping the statute of limitations has run out on that promise, Eleanor.

After writing all this stuff about science, I couldn't resist phoning my brother Dave, seeking hard evidence, so to speak, of that historical meeting with Louis St. Laurent. I asked him what, if anything, old Uncle Louie had said when he touched the heads of those two little boys that memorable day. Dave was delighted to remember; he remembered the whole day in detail, his friendship with Sid in more detail and was well into an analysis of the politics of Newfoundland's entrance into confederation, when I insisted: "David. David! What did he *say*?"

David laughed. "He said, 'keep it up, boys; keep it up.'"

We both laughed. He, I suppose, because of the pure banality of the words, I because I felt there could be no more appropriate double entendre to end this little meditation on politics and history than the idea that boys were told by the great leader of all of the Canadas to "keep it up." Indeed, in my humble woman's experience, they do indeed keep it up. All the clever arts and sciences and histories and literatures and the wild dances of politics and pornography help to "keep it up." And these discourses also help to keep me down. In all the ways culture lets women be and prevents us from being, in all the ways I manage to write myself into language and cannot write my self at all, and in all the daily ways I feel the weight of my imposterhood, I still live in that moment by the side of the road, on Craigmillar Avenue, back there in St. John's, Newfoundland, as the great man drives away.

Postscript

On the return journey of our trip to Newfoundland with which I began these memoirs, Richard and I stopped at what we Canadians—in imitation of our American neighbours—like to call "the nation's capital." I wanted Richard to see the new National Gallery and the spectacular Museum of Civilization. I had been to both a couple of times when I had gone to Ottawa to attend academic conferences, but he had not. He did not seem in the mood to be much of a tourist, but dutifully followed me about the gallery, and then tramped across the bridge to Hull for a look at the nation's new museum. We actually broke our long silence and exchanged words on the bridge to Quebec, laughing about how strange it will be, if the Québécois actually separate, to have to walk across a bridge to a foreign country to see our heritage. When he saw the sunshine colour of the Manitoba limestone that shapes the beautiful curves of the building and grounds of the museum, Richard reckoned that moving all that tonnage to the other side of the river would take a good bit of tax money. We laughed together. It seems that even a couple living in two solitudes can share the pleasure of a real Canadian joke.

The museum was as impressive as when I'd been there before, its architecture and its West Coast First Nations collection providing a breathtaking entrance with the promise of a rich history of our many-peopled land. This time I used one of-the museum's tape recorders to listen to the commentary on the Haida totems and the longhouses as I walked around the great monuments and through the homes of the first-comers. I learned a little of the language of the totems, of the families and histories that built them and the importance to a people's identity of Raven and the other animal figures that topped the poles. I wondered if Haida people visiting the museum might be a bit mystified by the prominence their heritage is given by the nation. A strange form of reparation.

By then I had lost sight of Richard and so moved on alone to the reconstructions of the first white settlements. I spent some time at the diaramas of the canny Acadians, making land out of sea marshes in the Maritimes at the beginning of the 1600s, inventing themselves as North Americans about the same time as my ancestors were discovering that cabbages managed very nicely in the skimpy soil of the Avalon. However, I found that the European first-comers to Newfoundland were pictured in the museum in the form of a diarama of those tough Basque sailors surviving the fishing season on the Grand Banks of Newfoundland, and a few hard winters in Placentia. I admired them and was very willing to share origins with them, but my people's early arrival was not noted. The museum's chronology leapt from Basques to all the later emigrations: the French settlement of Quebec, the arrival of the United Empire Loyalists from the rebel colonies and all the multicultural westwardness that followed, a westwardness that my husband's family were part of and in some ways, I felt a part of, too.

It was a story I knew well from my education as a Canadian, but on this visit the image of that jut of land at Crocker's Cove and all my folk who began their struggle in that Newfoundland place in the same times the Acadians began their struggle was still shining in my head from that ride around the bay and into our family's past.

But while the multiple origins of my country fit together just fine in my head, they were obviously not all fit for the makers of the museum of Canadian civilization. I was beginning to feel the loneliness of my Canadian identity again. My ancestors—unlike the First Nations peoples, unlike the Basque fishermen, unlike the Acadians, unlike the Québécois, my ancestors—with their fish flakes and their cabbages— were not part of the origins this national museum chronicles. As best as I could tell the Loyalists would seem to be the first English speakers. Newfoundland and its special separate history eventually does enter the museum's panorama of the story of Canada sometime around the same date that I, cradled by the maple leaves of my parents' garden, announced to the four corners of the earth that I was a Canadian. My ancestors are not yet inducted into the national story. Maybe the museum is waiting to see if we are merely a flash in the Canadian pan. But I trust my nation's continuing propensity for revision to bring us around to the early settlement of Newfoundland sooner or later. I am not so sure that the larger revision of culture will come so quickly around to the gender consciousness I would want. I have a good imagination, but I cannot yet imagine that.

As far as a museum of Canadian civilization is concerned, I want more for the next generation than I have had. I want the museum to collect a multitude of histories, a plethora of voices, a whole babble of memoirs and organize it all in some clever multimedia way so that when my children and grandchildren come to the museum they can seam together their multiple origins. I like to imagine my niece, Margaret Clarke from Nova Scotia, coming one day to the nation's capital, to the museum that chronicles all the civilizations that have made themselves real in this country. She will check the index of choices and perhaps she will decide to see and hear about both those Acadian marshlands of her mother's people and the cabbages and fish flakes of her father's folk. Maybe by the time she visits she will have children who bring with them, as well as her heritages, whole other histories from other families. I think she should be able to take up all the threads of her history and pattern them as she wants with the history of many others in the museum. And as she does so, she should be learning a way to make an identity that does not portray women's lives as merely a backdrop to the histories of men. She should be given many possibilities of identity so she can make her own story.

Richard and I were both tired by the time we walked back over the bridge to Ottawa that day. One day to sample the culture-making at the centre of the idea of nation had been enough after our long journey to Newfoundland and back. He wanted to leave very early the next morning. I think he was a little tired of the East, of being a tourist. He figured that with twenty hours of hard driving we could be safely on the Prairies. With Newfoundland many more than twenty hours behind me, I opted to be up at dawn and away westward. And so we were.

Books in the Life Writing Series Published by Wilfrid Laurier University Press

Haven't Any News: Ruby's Letters from the Fifties
Edited by Edna Staebler
with an Afterword by Marlene Kadar
1995 / x + 165 pp. / ISBN 0-88920-248-6

"I Want to Join Your Club": Letters from Rural Children, 1900-1920
Edited by Norah L. Lewis
with a Preface by Neil Sutherland
1996 / xii + 250 pp. (30 b&w photos) / ISBN 0-88920-260-5

And Peace Never Came
Elisabeth M. Raab
with Historical Notes by Marlene Kadar
1996 / x + 196 pp. (12 b&w photos, map) / ISBN 0-88920-281-8

Dear Editor and Friends: Letters from Rural Women of the North-West, 1900-1920
Edited by Norah L. Lewis
1998 / xvi + 166 pp. (20 b&w photos) / ISBN 0-88920-287-7

The Surprise of My Life: An Autobiography
Claire Drainie Taylor
with a Foreword by Marlene Kadar
1998 / ISBN 0-88920-302-4
xii + 268 pp. (+ 8 colour photos and 92 b&w photos)

Memoirs from Away: A New Found Land Girlhood
Helen M. Buss / Margaret Clarke
1998 / xvi + 153 pp. / ISBN 0-88920-314-8